imagining
the
future

imagining
the
future

Contributors
John Quinn • Mike Cooley • Jim Power • Tina Roche
Catherine Byrne • Archbishop Diarmuid Martin
Emily O'Reilly • Michael D. Higgins

EDITED BY HARRY BOHAN AND
GERARD KENNEDY

Our Society in the New Millennium

VERITAS

First published 2005 by
Veritas Publications
7/8 Lower Abbey Street
Dublin 1
Ireland
Email publications@veritas.ie
Website www.veritas.ie

ISBN 1 85390 804 5

Cover artwork by Avid Design
Printed in the Republic of Ireland by Betaprint, Dublin

*Veritas books are printed on paper made from the wood pulp of managed
forests. For every tree felled, at least one tree is planted, thereby renewing
natural resources.*

Contents

Contributors

John Quinn is a well-known broadcaster who retired from RTÉ Radio in December 2002 after a twenty-five year career, during which he won various awards at home and in Tokyo and New York. An established writer of children's fiction (he won the Bisto Book of the Year Award 1992) he has also edited several other acclaimed publications. In February 2003, he was awarded an honorary doctorate by the University of Limerick. John is a director of The Céifin Centre.

Jim Power joined Friends First Group in 2000 as Chief Economist and Director of Investment Strategy. He is a non-executive director and investment consultant to F&C (Ireland) Limited. He worked for the AIB group from 1979 to 1991 in Retail Banking, Strategic Planning and Group Treasury, where he was the Treasury Economist. He joined Bank of Ireland in 1991 as Senior Economist. He was appointed Chief Economist in 1995, and a Director in Treasury & International in 1998. He holds a BA in Economics and Politics, and a Master of Economic Science Degree from University College, Dublin. He currently lectures in Finance at Dublin City University. He is a frequent contributor to Irish and UK media. He is a native of Waterford and is married with two young boys.

Mike Cooley was born in Tuam, Co Galway and studied engineering in Germany, Switzerland and England. He has a PhD in Computer Aided Design. He is known to a wide audience in Ireland through his RTE broadcasts for *The Open Mind* and his six part series *Ways of Knowing*. He is an accomplished linguist, has broadcast on German TV and radio and undertaken specialist book translations. He is a consultant to a number of governments and international companies and is implementing economic development programmes in several countries. He is president of the International Research Institute in Human Centred Systems. He writes for publications worldwide and has made several films on high technology and its implications including one on the Equinox Series on Channel 4. His awards and distinctions include the Keys of the City of Osaka, the Freedom of the City of Detroit and the $50,000 Alternative Nobel Prize, which he donated to Socially Useful Production.

Tina Roche MBA is Chief Executive of The Foundation for Investing in Communities which has two divisions; Business in the Community, and The Community Foundation for Ireland. Tina has supported the agenda on Corporate Social Responsibility through the establishment of Business in the Community. She has overseen the development of the Schools Business Partnership, The Linkage Programme and Business Action on Homelessness. Tina is also leading the establishment of a permanent civic endowment fund through the development of The Community Foundation for Ireland. Tina previously worked for The National Gallery as Head of Development 1994-1999 and *The Sunday Tribune* as Head of Finance from 1983 to 1994. Her main interest is in human rights, education, community activism and social capital. She served on the executive board of Amnesty International Irish Section as Treasurer from 1992-1998 and is a current member. Tina is also a member of the senate of the NUI.

Catherine Byrne is currently the General Treasurer and Deputy General Secretary of the Irish National Teachers' Organisation (INTO), which has a membership of over 30,000 teachers. Catherine joined the INTO in 1981 as the first woman official and has over 20 years experience as a full-time officer in areas such as Equal Opportunities, Press and Publications, Professional Development and Training and Salary Negotiations. Catherine is a former trade union official with the European Trade Union Confederation, based in Brussels from 1991-1994 as Equal Opportunities Officer, and was the Irish representative on the European Network on Positive Action for Women in Employment from 1994-1996. She was a member of the second Irish Government Commission on the Status of Women.

Diarmuid Martin is the Catholic Archbishop of Dublin. He was appointed Coadjutor Archbishop of Dublin on 3 May 2003 and automatically succeeded Cardinal Desmond Connell as Archbishop of Dublin on 26 April 2004 when it was announced that Pope John Paul II had accepted Cardinal Connell's resignation. He was a member of various Vatican Offices, including the Central Committee for the Great Jubilee of the Year 2000. In March 2001 he was elevated to the rank of Archbishop and undertook responsibilities as Permanent Observer of the Holy See in Geneva, at the United Nations Office and Specialised Agencies and at the World Trade Organisations. During his service at the Pontifical Council for Justice and Peace, Archbishop Martin represented the Holy See at the major United Nations International Conferences on social questions held in the 1990s.

Emily O'Reilly was appointed Ireland's third Ombudsman on 1 June 2003 by the president of Ireland, Mrs Mary McAleese, on the nomination of each of the Houses of the Oireachtas (Dail and Seanad). Prior to her appointment, Ms O'Reilly was a journalist and author and had been a political correspondent for various media since 1989. The new Ombudsman was also appointed Ireland's second Information Commissioner under the Freedom of Information Act, 1997 on 1 June 2003. In this role Ms O'Reilly provides an independent review of decisions relating to the right of access of members of the public to records held by public bodies. She is also a member of the Standards in Public Office Commission, which was set up under the Ethics in Public Office Act, 1995 and of the Dail Constituency Commission. Ms O'Reilly is a native of Tullamore, Co Offaly and is married with five children. She was educated at University College Dublin and Trinity College Dublin. She was also the recipient of a Nieman Fellowship in Journalism at Harvard University, Cambridge, USA.

Michael D. Higgins is president of the Labour Party and Honorary Professor at Large at the National University of Ireland, Galway, where he has served on the Faculties of Arts, Commerce, Celtic Studies and Law. A former Member of Galway County Council and an Alderman of Galway Borough Council, he has twice been Mayor of Galway.

He was a member of Seanad Éireann 1973-1977; Dáil representative for Galway West 1981-1982, University Member of Seanad Éireann 1982-1987, and has been a Member of Dáil Éireann from 1987-present. He was the first Minister for Arts, Culture and the Gaeltacht, between 1993 and 1997, and President of the Council of Broadcasting Ministers of the European Union during the Irish Presidency of the European Union in 1996.

At different periods he has been Labour Party Spokesperson on European and International Affairs, Overseas Development,

Education and the Gaeltacht. He is currently a member of the Oireachtas Committee on Foreign Affairs and is Spokesperson on Foreign Affairs for the Labour Party.

Michael D. Higgins has campaigned for human rights in many parts of the world, including Turkey, Western Sahara, Nicaragua, Chile, Gaza, the West Bank, Peru, El Salvador, Iraq and East Timor. In recognition of his work for peace with justice in many parts of the world he became the first recipient of the Seán MacBride Peace Prize of the International Peace Bureau in Helsinki in 1992.

Michael D is married to Sabina Coyne, a founder member of The Focus Theatre and Stanislavsky Studio in Dublin. They have one daughter and three sons.

Introduction

HARRY BOHAN

Experience and history tell us that if at all possible we should avoid making the same mistake twice. Ireland was transformed economically in the 1960s, but the mistake made was to drive on commercially and allow market values to take over at the expense of values that give meaning to life. As a result seeds were sown for many of the problems that followed. For example, we built high-rise flats and massive housing estates, many of which eventually became unemployment blackspots. We are doing exactly the same again.

The fact is that market values are central to business and commercial life, but inappropriate when they over-influence certain professions such as medicine and law, or when they exploit young people, push family life to the sidelines and generally take over or swamp human and spiritual values.

The Céifin Centre, from the first conference in 1998 *Are We Forgetting Something?* to the *Imagining the Future* conference in 2004, has been trying to identify issues which need to be taken into account if the human, social and spiritual dimensions of life are to be taken seriously. The papers from this seventh annual conference published in this book will hopefully make some contribution to the debate about the direction Irish society is taking. The changes that have been taking place at such a rapid pace are extraordinary.

Economically, an under-achieving economic entity has been turned around to the extent that Ireland is now one of the materially wealthiest countries in the world. Socially, the Irish are now questioning as never before, and the previously sacrosanct position of the pillars of the community – the Church, the business elite and the political firmament – has been subjected to a level of scrutiny that would have been unimaginable in the Ireland of old. Culturally, Ireland has been transformed from a mono-ethnic society, to one where there is now a vast richness of ethnic diversity. Most of the change has been for the better, but it is clear that Ireland will face many challenges as it continues along the road of a modern, wealthy post-industrial society.

The last period of such immense change in Ireland was the 1960s. That decade witnessed three revolutions – industrial, communications and education – which fundamentally altered the face of Ireland and of Irish life in general. The growing pressures on the traditional family and community and their values, together with other significant challenges to moral principles, indicated abandonment of social norms long respected, with little consideration for the long-term effects of their abandonment. Ireland was becoming part of the wider world, but at the expense of disconnecting from the local. In a practical way, the village communities in Ireland together with their hinterlands, had been losing their population to centres at home – mainly to massive urban housing estates and to high-rise flats.

RHO (Rural Housing Organisation) was formed in 1972 to address the problems and issues that followed that decade of dramatic change. At a time when government was closing Garda barracks, rural schools, and post offices and when the attractions of urban living were being marketed aggressively, RHO began a housing programme for young couples in villages. This movement spread into one hundred and twenty villages in thirteen counties, resulting in the direct construction of two and a half thousand houses. The achievement was to restore a balanced population, and give renewed life to rural schools, shops, churches, social organisations and community building in general. This movement eventually evolved into a wider community development movement, sowing the seeds for a significant rural development programme in Europe, which took the form of the LEADER Programme. LEADER is now actively involved in maintaining the vibrancy and life of rural communities.

The RHO movement evolved into the foundation of the Céifin Centre for Values-Led Change. It ran its first conference entitled, *Are We Forgetting Something?* in 1998 and has successfully run six subsequent conferences focusing on the issues and challenges confronting an economy and a society that has been transformed so dramatically in such a short period of time. The aim of the annual conference is to stimulate debate on issues that are identified as being fundamental to the stability and soundness of Irish society going forward. These issues include:

- The breakdown of authority
- The disconnection from the inner self
- The growing trend of marriage breakdown
- The decline of agriculture as a way of life
- The migration of people to urban centres and the creation of a 'dormitory' rural community
- The impact that wealth creation has had on Irish society
- Substance abuse and violent crime
- The regeneration of economic life in rural Ireland
- The challenge of globalisation
- The role of business in the community.

These are just some of the issues discussed at the seven annual conferences, which have been attended by a significant cross-section of Irish life, and have been addressed by a distinguished panel of domestic and international speakers. The key aim is to ensure that the subjects discussed at the Céifin conference become influential in driving national debate.

The Céifin Centre has also held conferences on sport, spirituality, and parenting, and has carried out significant research on: family life, well-being and stress in the workplace, and the future of Catholic education – both primary and secondary. The proposed title for the 2005 annual conference is *Filling the Vacuum*. The key theme of the conference will be to explore the concept and role of *community* in the evolving Irish economy. In addition to having speakers with vision around this concept of community, it is intended to invite people at community level to tell their stories of action at this level. This is a clear recognition that the community is once again creating the balance in our society, in other words demonstrating the power of the local in the face of powerful global influences. In many ways this will bring Céifin right back to where RHO started in the 1970s. The focus is once again on action at local level. We believe that this is appropriate because of the speed at which the Irish economy and society are changing and the pressures that are placed upon local communities. We would hope to start a national debate on the importance of increased participation at local level in order to improve the quality of life for every citizen of Ireland.

Filling the vacuum? Who is attempting to do that? There is obviously a vacuum in our society, which is not seriously addressed by religious or secular organisations. People are uneasy, many live in fear, some are discontented and growing numbers have given up altogether. The relentless drive for economic growth, the power of a money culture, the values underpinning both are now determining how we live and leaving too many empty and frustrated. What is happening to family and community? Are we moving towards elitism in sport, with more and more becoming armchair participants? Have we too many 'chaplains' in religion and not enough 'prophets' and 'witnesses'? And what of the media? These will all be explored in the 2005 conference.

This will follow on from one of the most powerful messages of the November 2004 conference *Imagining the Future*; this message being that it is time to pause, time to give serious thought as to how we are connecting at local level. The speakers at this last conference were Emily O'Reilly (*Imagining the Future – An Irish Perspective*), Michael D. Higgins (*Imagining the Future – The Global Perspective*), Archbishop Diarmuid Martin (*Imagining the Future for Organised Religion*), Catherine Byrne (*Imagining the Future – For Our Schools*), Mike Cooley (*Imagining the Future – For Our Young People*) and Tina Roche (*Imagining the Future in a Socially Responsible Business World*). In his *View from the Chair*, Jim Power has outlined the key messages contained in each paper. The overall message is contained in Emily O'Reilly's much quoted paper:

> The deeply, heartfelt hope that our children would have better lives, and in the context of this shiny new wealthy Ireland, that that better life has to do not with the accumulation of stuff, but with an awareness of the true meaning of a rich life, of a life where the pleasures of love, of companionship, of reading, of art, of sharing one's gifts, of seeking to obtain ever higher understanding of the mysteries, beauties and even ugliness that surround us are really all that matter.

Debates like this certainly help us to face the future with confidence and in the knowledge that there are people around Ireland giving serious thought to the challenges facing us.

The Céifin Centre for Values-Led Change is happy to provide a forum for this debate and for bringing people together who in turn will bring some of the ideas exchanged back to their own locality.

We are deeply grateful once again to all the people who attended our conference. We are indebted to the speakers for their excellent presentations and in particular to Michael D Higgins who willingly participated at very short notice when John Pilger was unable to travel due to illness. We were very fortunate to have two exceptional Chairpeople, John Quinn and Jim Power who did a terrific job and for that we thank them.

On the organisational side we would like to thank Máire Johnston and Susan Ward, conference co-ordinators, our volunteers and conference committee who gave so generously of their time. To the management and staff of the West County Hotel we extend our gratitude. To our sponsors, particularly Waterford Crystal, we are very grateful.

We are also grateful for the considerable coverage of the event in the media as well as the promotional work done on behalf of the conference by Nicky Woulfe.

We at the Céifin Centre believe that we are making a significant contribution to the national debate on issues that are fundamental to the future well-being of Irish society, and we intend to continue with this work.

A View From The (Arm) Chair

John Quinn

I first discovered Mike Cooley over twenty years ago in a lecture-hall in University College Dublin when he electrified a packed audience with an animated discussion on 'The Future of Work'. Since then I featured him regularly (and unapologetically!) on RTE Radio and always to much acclaim. His ideas and his communicative skills won him a faithful audience. For me it was the sheer breadth of his vision that ultimately made him my mentor and my friend. When I proposed to the Board of Céifin that 'Imagining Our Future' should be the theme of the 2004 conference I further stipulated that Mike Cooley should give the keynote address. Happily, the board ran with both ideas. I hope that those who were lucky enough to attend the conference and those who will read its proceedings will feel I was vindicated. In a technology-driven world Mike Cooley's voice is one of sanity, humaneness and vision, celebrating human intelligence and ingenuity in all its many forms and traditions. It is a voice that needs to be heard.

To mark Ireland's presidency of the European Union in 2004 the then Minister for Education Noel Dempsey TD commissioned me to put together a book that would 'celebrate learning and teaching'. A noble and admirable idea. I was very flattered to be asked, but initially unsure if I could deliver. It occurred to me that with a career of over twenty-five years in broadcasting I had been privileged to encounter a wide range of people who had interesting ideas on learning and teaching. Here was an opportunity to distil many of those ideas into print. I remembered specifically a series I had done with Mike Cooley entitled 'Ways of Knowing'. The series traced his own career and the development of his ideas and it made the basic point that there are many ways of knowing our world. And so *Ways of Knowing* became both the title and the theme of the 2004 book. It is a most handsome book with elegant photographs by Tom Lawlor, but for me the delight was found in bogman Johnny Kelly's knowledge of his own environment simply by being in it and absorbing all it had to offer; in Eilis Brady's love and lore of street-games; in Séan Ó Faoláin's lyrical evocation of 'doing nothing' on his Auntie Nan's farm; in Walter McGinitie's essay on 'the power of uncertainty'; in Jim Deeny's affirmation that 'it takes a village to raise a child'... and many more instances, including the learning experiences of Mike Cooley. The book was not a commercial publication but the Department of Education were so pleased with it that they sent a copy to every school in the country.

Mike Cooley's ideas were very much the seedbed of that book. It was truly a delight – twenty years on – to hear Mike put those ideas to the Céifin conference with, if anything, even more passion and belief and it was a privilege to then engage with him in a public 'armchair discussion'. For this publication Mike Cooley has expertly distilled his address and the armchair deliberations into a forceful and visionary treatment of what 'education' might be. It is an extremely important paper and together with the other contributions –

particularly Emily O'Reilly's riveting assessment of our society today it should be readily available to every second-level student in the country. Is there, I earnestly ask, a benefactor out there who would place a copy of this book in every second-level school? Just imagine the seeds you would sow...

Imagining the Future for our Young People

MIKE COOLEY

(This is an extract from Mike Cooley's presentation at the Céifin 2004 Conference.)

The year 2000 represented the end of the most extraordinary millennium in human history, certainly from a Eurocentric viewpoint. The great physicist, Heisenberg said: 'Prediction is very difficult, particularly about the future.' The implication is that predictions about the past are also very difficult, because we invent and reinvent, revisit and understand the past in different ways in the course of our history.

Within that millennium we have seen the decline in feudalism, the growth of capitalism, the development of an industrial society, the growth of vast urban conurbations. We have also seen science replace religion as the driving force in society. We have seen the replacement of belief by so-called fact. Underlying all of this has been a shift from right and wrong to convenience and inconvenience. These changes have profound implications as to how we understand ourselves today and the kind of future we might desire.

Double Edged

The underlying technological development that made these changes possible has always been double-edged. It resulted in the beauty of the construction of Venice on the one hand, and the hideousness of the Chernobyl disaster on the other. It facilitated the therapeutic and diagnostic potential of Roentgen's X-rays, but related technologies gave rise to the destruction of Hiroshima.

The future which I envisage for young people is one in which we should develop the capacity to identify and build upon the positive features of technology and seek to marginalise negative features. The laws of thermodynamics show us that we don't get something for nothing. There is always a price to pay for progress and there are no free dinners. Technological change is usually portrayed as a universal good and a 'win-win' situation. In consequence, we often fail to deal with, or even consider its multiplier effects and how best to cope with these.

Beautiful Experience

The change in our society has been so rapid that it is difficult to understand even when you are in the centre of the action. Looking back, you will see that wheeled transport existed in much the same form for a thousand years. Watts's steam engine continued to work 102 years after it was built. Fixed capital in the 1930s was written off in twenty-five years. Today, even as we design new products they are already becoming obsolete. The rate of change is bewildering. Thus if somebody qualified as a physicist twenty-five years ago and had not updated their knowledge in the meantime, they would find themselves in the same quartile as Pythagoras and Archimedes. The idea that schools and universities can provide young people with a tool-kit of knowledge and competence to use for the rest of their lives is obviously no longer valid. Rather, we should encourage our young people to retain a childlike curiosity, a learning habit and a sense of the mysterious. As Einstein put it:

> The most beautiful experience we can have is the mysterious. It is the fundamental emotion which stands at the cradle of true art and true science. Whoever does not know it and can no longer wonder, no longer marvel, is as good as dead.

Awesome Capacity

The rate of change in the last hundred years alone has been mind blowing. We learned to fly, we killed 40,000,000 people in one war, we called Jackson Pollack a great artist and we played golf on the moon. We are the first generation of the only species we know of that has it within its power to destroy itself and our beautiful planet. This is an awesome capacity and we are ill-equipped educationally and otherwise to deal with it.

So we clearly perceive ourselves to be an upwardly mobile species. Yet at no stage in human history have so many people felt frightened by and alienated from the society in which they live. I now believe that we have become far too smart scientifically to survive much longer without wisdom.

Most Precious Asset

Gradually, what we are seeing is people becoming more like machines and machines more like people. The loss of identity arising from this is deeply problematic. The famous Turing test was introduced about sixty years ago so that we could distinguish between a human being and a computer. Modern technology results in a convergence between them. What we need instead is a symbiosis – a living together of both based on the best attributes of each. Part of the way of achieving that symbiosis would be to design systems which support, enhance and celebrate human intelligence.

The most precious asset any society, country or culture has is the skill, ingenuity, creativity and imagination of its people. This may have seemed self-evident a few years ago. However the discussion nowadays is already underway as to whether we should still regard human beings as an asset to be developed and enhanced, or whether we should perceive them as a burden to be dispensed with like an obsolete machine which becomes too expensive to run.

The systems which provide for this reductionist way of thinking are themselves becoming mechanised. You only have to look at the rituals teachers are expected to go through with the myriad of so-called tests. One of my facetious laws of computing states: 'Any teacher who can be replaced by a computer deserves to be.' If any professionals so diminish what they do and no longer bring imagination, ingenuity and intentionality to their tasks, they diminish themselves in the face of the systems they are producing.

An AI expert recently stated succinctly and brutally: 'Human beings will have to accept their true place in the evolutionary hierarchy; animals, human beings and intelligent machines.' Unless we have the wisdom and the imagination to develop countervailing designs, this really will become a self-fulfilling prophecy.

Things We Know But Cannot Tell
The future I envisage for our young people is one in which their capacity to judge and imagine will be encouraged and treasured. As matters stand our society is moving in the opposite direction and there is a drastic shift from judgement to calculation. We are told we are in an information society and are now becoming a knowledge society, but I would question such a theory. I believe we are in a data society. Transforming data into information is a meaningful human activity. Applying this information in a domain becomes knowledge which, absorbed in a culture, can result in wisdom leading to appropriate action.

At the knowledge/wisdom/action end we find tacit knowledge. This is the type of knowledge to which the philosopher of science Michael Polanyi referred when he said, 'There are things we know but cannot tell'. Tacit knowledge incorporates the sense of size, shape, form and appropriateness which comes from working on the real world around us. Together with some colleagues I have demonstrated that it is possible to design systems – we refer to them as 'Human Centred Systems' – operating in this tacit area and which are much more amenable to human beings.

Dramatic Example
In spite of this, our educational system continues to overemphasise the significance of data ('facts') which have not been tempered by a process of experience. This places the emphasis on propositional knowledge ('know that') as opposed to tacit knowledge ('know how'). In consequence of the growing emphasis on the former we are losing our ability to judge and are increasingly reliant (some would say abjectly so) on calculation. I could bore you with instances of the consequences of this but let me give you one example as evidence.

Two paediatricians in England were working out the dose of morphine for a child. Their basic procedure was correct, namely they measure the body mass of the child and then multiplied this figure by the medication per-unit-mass. However, in doing so, they misplaced the decimal point which resulted in their prescribing a dose of morphine one hundred times the appropriate amount. A nurse happened to see this and pointed out that it simply could not be right, but the paediatricians administered it in any case and the child was killed almost instantly.

Prefigured by a Poet
The human-centred systems I mentioned earlier, provide tools which support and enhance human skill and ingenuity rather

than replacing it by calculation alone. It is difficult to describe the issues involved here and I was surprised when one of my colleagues pointed out that he had seen a similar theory at work in a poem by T S Eliot. It was interesting that issues of this kind which we were currently grappling with, could have been prefigured by a poet. Sure enough, in his collection, *Voices from the Rocks*, Eliot says:

> …and where is the wisdom we have lost in knowledge?
> Where is the knowledge we have lost in information?
> Where is the life we have lost in living?

So often, the big issues in society and in science and technology are prefigured by culture, music, literature and poetry. In the future I envisage these forms would be treasured and respected as highly among young people as the abilities in science and technology. Furthermore, it should be a future in which we respect a whole variety of learning abilities and individual learning styles, one in which there will be a possible symbiosis of the formal and informal, the explicit and implicit.

Informal Learning
In most instances students travel through a rather conventional education system from secondary schools and onto university, graduating without much practice in the work place. Conversely there are those who gain their knowledge through informal learning and have acquired implicit knowledge.

May I suggest as examples people like Michael Smurfit and Ray MacSharry in Ireland or Richard Branson, Alan Sugar or Sir Alex Ferguson in the UK. In a recent analysis of the characteristics and attributes of five thousand 'self made' millionaires in Britain it was clear that they certainly didn't constitute a group of people who achieved a traditional education.

People acquire their abilities in all sorts of diverse ways and they demonstrate them in unorthodox and sometimes even unacceptable actions. In this context, the press often emphasise the destructiveness and even the criminality of young people particularly in urban areas. However, another aspect of this is that these young people often demonstrate extraordinary skills in these unacceptable activities. A recent television programme demonstrated how a group of young car thieves were able to break into a car, get it started and drive away in less than a minute. I sometimes find it difficult to do so even when I've got the correct set of keys.

An experimental project in North East London encouraged youngsters of this kind to become involved in a car conversion project where cars could be retro-fitted with an electrical drive. Although this was only a demonstration project it did show the extraordinary energy and imagination of these young people and it behoves society to hold out to them an opportunity to give vent to their tacit knowledge and ability. To do this we must understand that these young people demonstrate their knowledge through what they do and how they do it, rather than through writing and talking about it.

Learning by doing

Another product was this marvellous chair for severely disabled children who each require a closely fitting chair to support their body at the point of weakness. Since the child is constantly growing he or she outgrows the chair every six months. To overcome this, a variable geometric seat was designed, which was adjustable in all directions and would 'grow' with the child. Activities of this kind make superb 'Learning by Doing' projects.

I hope you will share my belief that there are many different ways of articulating intelligence. We must avoid confusing linguistic ability with intelligence and recognise that there are skills which cannot be set down easily in writing but are best expressed by making and doing socially useful things.

This can also have a tremendous humanising effect on young people who, in our industrial society, are being increasingly dehumanised. Some of the children working on these projects were real rough and tumble kids but were greatly taken by the fact that they could actually help other people and contribute to society.

Nowadays, to paraphrase Oscar Wilde, we appear to know the price of everything and the value of nothing. In contrast, there is a deep strain of humanity in all of us, which society, at the moment, is ignoring. There are mechanisms which we could develop that would allow us to take action and build upon that tacit knowledge. People actually do get fulfilment and enjoyment from helping others.

The Abolition of Childhood

Youth is very fleeting yet its imprint stays with us most of our lives. I deplore the growing abolition of childhood. By that I mean the attempt by society to pre-programme people and to deny them the basic human right of developing their own attributes and skills. Young people are being programmed earlier and earlier. It has now come to the stage in the United States that there is a company selling a sonic device that can be used to re-programme the foetus while it is still in the womb.

We now have a society where young people are unable to play on the roads and are afraid to go to parks. As a result of this, children don't go out. Remember the film *Home Alone?* We now have the phenomenon of 'Home Alone Together'. The ruthless individualism that society imposes means that families at home won't even share a meal. Instead they feed from the fridge, watch different television programmes and fail to undertake joint activities of any kind.

Some families no longer have a dining table. One family I know of had to hire a table when the grandparents came for Christmas so that they would have some place to eat their

Christmas dinner together. This would be laughable were it not so tragic.

Big Issues on a Small Scale

I had this gifted childhood in Tuam. It was the grain of sand in which I could see the whole world. It allowed me to deal with big issues on a very small scale but above all, it allowed time to play. Play was not seen as a diversion from the seriousness of study. It was something we all did and it was remarkably fulfilling. We had one game where we would select a stone or a piece of deadwood and each of us would say what we saw in it. The different things people saw in the grain was fascinating – the eye of a greyhound, the shape of a gnarled fist or a skull. We would visualise the various objects that could be made from the stone. It is said that Michelangelo could already see the figure of David in the unworked piece of marble. He then removed 'all that was not David' and so David emerged. In our simple unconscious way we were laying the basis of a 'David moment' of our own.

We used to sit around in circles and tell stories. I guess young people still do that. I don't know. We would each agree to tell a story and try to make the others cry. Of course, everyone would tell a story about a dear one who had died. Tom Murphy, later to become the famous playwright, suggested that somebody dying as a basis to move others should not be allowed, so we had to be more creative. I remember that one of my stories was about a beloved shawl used to keep a sick child warm. It fell into the Ballygaddy River was washed over the waterfall and disappeared. The others were really moved by this story.

We used to play a lot near local rivers. Making small restrictions in the flow of water fascinated me. As a little leaf boat passed through the gap I could see it accelerating. Years later I learned that this is known as the Venturi Phenomenon. In industry, when I was working on a cardio-vascular diagnostic device, to find the rate of change of blood flow, one of my colleagues said, 'Mike, you have an extraordinary intuitive knowledge of hydrodynamics'. 'I haven't actually,' I replied. 'I used to play with water.' It really is true that you get insights from a closeness to nature. Watching the salmon coming back in the salmon weir in Galway with my uncle Martin made me wonder how they could have guided themselves back to the same place. If they were deep below the water, could they see the light of the stars and if it was overcast were they guided by magnetic fields? The imagination raced.

All of those childhood experiences informs later work I did on control systems. And then there was the moon. I was always fascinated by the moon and I feel so sorry for young people who never have the opportunity of being out at night and experiencing the sheer delight of it all.

Critical, I believe in all these matters, is motivation, and as John Quinn and others have pointed out, motivation is stimulated by imagination. You see, if you are highly motivated and adults support and encourage you, it is quite extraordinary where it will lead. I decided at the age of fourteen that I wanted to learn German. I had seen these newsreels with Hitler ranting and I had also begun to appreciate classical German music. I wondered how a nation that had all this culture could be responsible for all these unspeakable atrocities. I felt I had to learn that language to try and understand. Franz Kaplan, from Vienna, was the engineering manager of the Tuam sugar factory. I insisted that his wife teach me German. By the time I was eighteen I could speak fluent German. Now Tuam is not a centre of Germanic studies, but if you have the determination to pursue things, it is amazing how you can create your own educational network. I always point out that I *learned* German rather than studied it.

DIY Comprehensive Education
I was attending the Christian Brothers' school and doing well there. However, I wanted to expand my horizons. I asked if it

would be possible to take each Wednesday afternoon off and go to the local 'Tech' where I could study technical drawing and metalwork. I always remember Brother Rafferty going white with concern when I told him I would leave the Christian Brothers altogether and go to the tech if they didn't agree. He said: 'Michael, if you go to that place you will be finished. Only the children from Tuberjarlath Road go there'. He didn't refer to it as a school and had used Tuberjarlath to hammer home the point that it was a poor, dilapidated and undesirable part of town. The Christian Brothers wouldn't agree to my proposed comprehensive education so I left them and went to the tech with the backing of my parents. The following year Tom Murphy experienced the same reaction and he too left.

I often speculate that if he had continued at the Christian Brothers where he was doing quite well, got his Leaving Cert in the appropriate subjects and went on to TCD, he may well have ended up writing the same boring, arid, grammatical English as the rest of us. His delight in the human voice and the beauty of descriptive language might not have developed and Irish theatre might not have soared so splendidly to the heights of *The Gigli Concert*.

Transcendence

This episode emphasised for me the obsession with 'the one best way' and the inability of institutions to see that truly motivated people have an extraordinary way of marshalling capabilities and reserves of skill to undertake something. The education system generally ignores the importance of intentionality and purpose, all of which lay the basis for that extraordinary human attribute – transcendence. This is the ability to recognise mechanisms and processes which allow us to go beyond the present state of things.

The great historical example of transcendence is the building of the Cupola of Santa Maria del Fiore by Brunelleschi. It is the most complicated structure in Christendom. Brunelleschi served his time as a goldsmith. When he had finished his seven-year apprenticeship, which he had started at the age of twelve, he was asked if he could make the kind of chalices which he was then engraving. He was then asked to make the tabernacles to enclose the chalices and later the altars to surround the tabernacles. Eventually he was contracted to make the churches to surround the altars. Having started out as a goldsmith, he ended up designing and building the biggest structure in Christendom. This is real career progression and there wasn't a human resource development manager in sight. What did exist, however, was a culture of transcendence.

Not given only, but taken

They used to talk about the Wanderjahre, where you would wander out and acquire skills – rather like a journeyman. That is in the essence of education. Education in my view, like democracy, cannot really be given. It has to be taken. Taking it is part of the process.

Yet our schools condition young people in many cases in quite the opposite direction. We should realise that people can flourish and develop in environments that are quite different to the ones we, as educationalists, think desirable for them.

Just imagine the real case of a young person at fifteen, disastrous at school, disruptive and a misfit. Nobody could imagine what to do with him. Eventually, they had to try and find some employment for him. The only thing they could find for him to do was to work at home with his mother, who was a seamstress. That was Versace! In a film on his life he described how his mother showed him how to get fabrics to flow around the human body. It laid the foundations for his glittering career. When Versace died, his business turnover was $582 million a year, yet many educationalists would have thought that this lack of schooling would be the end of that child's prospects.

What I am urging you to contemplate is the idea of a great diversity of capabilities. We should not be obsessed with exams.

There are many other ways we could begin to judge young people. Exams essentially find out what you don't know rather than what you do. There used to be a tradition at Cambridge, that if you didn't like the question the examiner set you could ignore it and answer your own question. That should be a vital part of the future; a society where people have the courage and imagination to write their own questions.

Ways of Knowing

For me, one of the most moving programmes in my RTE series with John Quinn arose when he asked me to do a programme called Millennium Minds. I recall that all the others chose their millennium mind from this small Judeo-Christian corner of the world. I chose Chief Seattle of the Suquamish people in America because I had read a visionary statement attributed to him after his people were forced into a reservation. He was told that this move would constitute progress for his people. He made this moving speech, saying:

> Every part of this country is sacred to my people. Every valley, every hillside, every glade, is hallowed in the memory and experience of my tribe. Even the soil in which you stand responds more lovingly to our footsteps than to yours. For the soil is rich with the life of my people. Our religion exists in the hearts and the minds of our people. Your religion was written on tablets of stone by the iron finger of an angry God.

He also reportedly said:

> The Great White Chief at Washington wishes to buy our land. We cannot understand this concept. How do you buy a ripple on a stream? How do you buy the freshness of the wind as it weaves through the trees?

We need such insights to inform the debate as environmental disasters continue to bear in on us.

The Half Full Glass

I think it is always constructive to try and emphasise what people do know rather than what they don't know and to consider what motivates them, so you can build on that. However, in many cases our system tends to do the opposite. That destructiveness is so beautifully prefigured in James Joyce's *Finnegan's Wake*, where he reminds us that we are all made up of the two different characteristics, Shem and Shaun, and of the negative one he says:

> Sniffer of carrion, premature gravedigger, seeker of the nest of evil in the bosom of a good word, you who sleep at our vigil and fast for our feast, you with your dislocated reason have reared your disunited kingdom on the vacuum of your own most intensely doubtful soul.

Successful Disobedience

Because of this 'most intensely doubtful soul' we are relying more and more on rule-based systems. These are held out as a sort of panacea in large corporations, local government, health care and of course in schools. I find it quite extraordinary!

The first thing any active trade unionist learns is that the way to stop everything in its tracks is by working to rule. It's all the little things we do outside the rules that keeps everything going. Uniformity and conformity are imposed at an earlier and earlier stage in our lives. Yet more perceptive employers now say that when selecting young people to build the future of their companies they need to look also for 'successful disobedience'. If we ever lose the capacity to work outside the rules we will indeed be in great difficulty.

I am frequently asked if I believe that 'ordinary people' can cope with the complexities now bearing in on us. I always point out that I have never succeeded in meeting an ordinary person. All the people I meet are quite extraordinary with all kinds of wishes, needs and intentionality which we should treasure and build upon. This will require the capacity to valorise diversity. It would be sad indeed if, now that we are beginning to understand the significance of biodiversity, we were to ignore the significance of cultural and linguistic diversity and, for example, succumb to the cultural imperialism of technocratic jargon. The starting point here in Ireland might be to pay more attention to our own descriptive native language.

A Fault in Reality

Industrial society is forever claiming that it is superb at giving us what we want. It seldom mentions what it is taking away. Its real talent lies in diverting us from imagining what we might want. The future I envisage for our young people will be one in which they are encouraged – even provoked – into embarking on that journey of imagination. As the students of the 60s used to say, 'Don't adjust your mind, there's a fault in reality'.

I would like to conclude by pointing out that the future is not 'already out there' in the sense that a coastline might be 'out there' before somebody discovers it. The future has no predetermined shape, form or contour. It has yet to be built and we all have real choices in shaping that very future.

A View From The Chair

JIM POWER

Since its inception the annual Céifin conference has established itself as an arena where issues are debated in a full and frank manner, and where ideas are batted by the speakers out into the audience and are returned with sometimes awesome power and ferocity. It is generally a pretty unfettered environment where all manner of ideas and visions are shared and discussed. It is one thing discussing diverse ideas, but it is another thing entirely to ensure that the ideas are promulgated to a wider audience and go some way towards shaping a broader national policy agenda.

The seventh annual Céifin conference got off to the worst possible start with the distressing news that the keynote speaker, John Pilger, would be unable to travel to Ennis due to illness. From the organisers' perspective this presented an immense challenge, but thanks to the quality of speakers already lined up alongside John Pilger, and an able stand in, in the shape of Michael D Higgins, the organisers need not have worried. The conference turned out to be a very strong and thought provoking affair, and one that thankfully gained considerable media attention in the weeks following the event.

As an economist who occupies a world of concrete statistics and models, the prospect of chairing a conference with the nebulous title 'Imagining the Future', posed a daunting prospect. In the event I probably should not have been too concerned as the calibre of the speakers carried the day and rendered the task of chairman quite easy and enjoyable. At one of the coffee breaks I overheard my chairing techniques attracting some stinging criticism on the basis that I cut off the question & answer session with some brutality. To me that criticism spoke volumes for the quality of the conference. From a Chairman's point of view and from the perspective of conference speakers and organisers in general, there is nothing more disappointing than a muted reaction to an address. The fact that I had to end the session prematurely to keep the conference on track is indicative of the reaction that all of the speakers elicited from the audience. That, in my humble view, is the ultimate testament to the success and quality of any conference.

Ireland has come a long way over the past couple of decades in terms of economic and social development, but more particularly in terms of the cultural diversity that now characterises the country. Some of the change has been positive and some has been negative, but it has all been momentous. As we look forward to the coming decades it is clear that the change that has occurred to date is only the tip of the iceberg. In considering where we will be as a country in twenty years time, we need to face up to the problems and challenges that confront us today and ensure that we try to address them in a sensible way and shape as good a future for our children as we possibly can.

The problems facing the country today are very different from those we faced twenty years ago and in many ways are issues associated with the economic and material success that we have enjoyed. We are now at a point in our development where power and authority have been seriously undermined, with the Church, business, and the political firmament all having suffered serious reputational damage in recent years. Having seen the 'pillars of authority' dismantled there is now a sense of vacuum that could lead to a very negative outcome if it is not filled in a sensible way. We need to act now to shape the manner in which the country is evolving. However, in order to shape the future we need to have some idea of what we would define as success ten or twenty years down the road. To do this would require a level of imagination that we have not displayed heretofore, but we should keep trying. Bringing together speakers from the Church, the trade union movement, a government agency, politics and business in order to try to elicit their view of the future represents a major step in the right direction.

Tina Roche opened the conference with a most interesting and stimulating discussion of the role of business in shaping the future, and the challenges of globalisation. She argued that the process of globalisation is not working for many, but that with a little imagination much can be achieved. She argued for the creation of meaningful jobs to help alleviate poverty, products that do no harm to the environment or the consumer, high occupational standards, sustainable production, gender balance and openness and transparency. These represent just some of the items on her long wish list, but to me one of her strongest messages was the interdependence of all of us in the face of the realities of globalisation, and the fact that business can be seen as a solution to problems.

Catherine Byrne then presented her vision of the school of the future. In case we needed reminding, she warned us that we should not glamorise the past too much, as it had many less than pleasant features in the educational arena, not least the abuse of power and corporal punishment. As somebody involved in a fund raising exercise in my sons' primary school to provide basic facilities that any civilised society should expect, I was particularly taken with her view that the pyramid should be inverted, with a much greater focus on primary education. In my view, education is the key to alleviating poverty and so it is imperative to ensure that a child's first exposure to the education system is a positive one. Her views on a holistic approach to education and the power of freethinking were also very sensible.

After taking our fill of caffeine, we returned to hear Archbishop Diarmuid Martin offer his views on the role of the church and organised religion in the future. While facing up to failures of the church in the past, he certainly did not give one the impression of a man who is going to beat himself up about those failures. He argued that the Church should be allowed to get on with its other duties despite the mistakes, and that the church as a 'communion of communities' has a key role to play in the future. He outlined his belief that organised religion will change, but will not go away. He also spoke strongly of the dominant role of alcohol in Irish society and the culture of violence that is now such a part of Irish life. The challenge for the church and indeed for all interested parties is to conquer this very undesirable facet of Irish life today.

Traditionally, the after lunch slot is viewed as the 'graveyard' slot, where the speaker struggles to keep both themselves and the audience awake. However, at the seventh Céifin conference, the 'graveyard' slot turned out to be anything but. Emily O'Reilly delivered a riveting exposition on many aspects of Ireland today, ranging from blatant consumerism to unrestrained drunkenness, to violence, to the 'childlike showing off of helicopters and four wheel drives and private cinemas', and much more besides. It was the most amazing and stunning exposition on modern Ireland that I have ever experienced. The reaction of the audience said it all and not surprisingly, she got the most deserving standing ovation I have ever witnessed. If we were worried by the lack of John Pilger, we need not have been because in my view, nothing he would have said could have overshadowed Emily. As a father of two young boys myself, what she described resonated strongly with me and I actually found the whole experience quite emotional. Enough said at this juncture, but everybody should read her article in full and make their own minds up on the quality of the content. A truly memorable experience!

The final speaker of the day was Michael D. Higgins, who was a last minute replacement for John Pilger. Michael D. delivered his usual erudite and poetic vision of life. His wide ranging presentation touched on many aspects of life and society, but his stressing of the need to question certainties was central to his overall theme.

So ended the latest Ceifin conference and despite the last minute withdrawal, it turned out to be a most stimulating and thought provoking experience. Emily O Reilly's thoughts have subsequently and not surprisingly attracted considerable media attention. She dared question why many of us still feel unfulfilled despite the many material advances we have made and my lasting memory of the day is her imagined obituary 'Here lies Mrs X, fifth in line for a Birkin Bag, and raging she wasn't first'. Emily used the opportunity presented at Céifin to 'ponder what we have become and what we want to become'. Hopefully all present did that and hopefully all present at the conference have at this stage fulfilled the commitment to go out and carry the ideas discussed at Céifin into the public arena.

Imagining the Future in a Socially Responsible Business World

TINA ROCHE

To begin I want to talk to you a little about what we do at Business in the Community and what we are, so you can place the following paper in context. We are a support organisation for businesses wishing to engage in the area of corporate responsibility. It is an ambitious undertaking and back at our office we have experts who specialise in this area and who support companies who wish to become more responsibly minded. This involves checking on what companies are doing in terms of corporate responsibility and suggesting ways in which they can improve. We also work with companies who engage with the local community on local or national issues. I will return to this later. We have three programmes centred around the area of social inclusion. The first programme involves placing homeless people, who are ready for work, in employment. We work with Marks and Spencer, and Anglo Irish Bank on this. Over the last eighteen months we have found meaningful placements for about fifty homeless people and we have learned a great deal as a result. The second programme focuses on building partnerships between schools and businesses. We knew that with the power of business we could bring about change in the area of education. On inspection we discovered from the Department of Education that 10,000 children leave school every year without a leaving certificate qualification. What schools are affected by that? We got a list of 107 schools right across the country. What we decided to do was see if we could make an impact on reducing those figures. To date we have matched about 47 of the 107 schools with businesses in order to offer mentoring and skills at work for students, and management excellence programmes for principals where we talk about leadership, performance management, staff engagement and stakeholder dialogue.

In addition, we began placing ex-offenders in employment four years ago as a result of those who approached us and asked for assistance. Given the nature and title of our company they believed we could make contacts for them with possible employers. So we decided to set a target of thirty. Could we place thirty ex-offenders in employment in one year and could we, as a company, learn through the experience? At the time I thought it would be impossible that employers would give these people a second chance, but I am delighted to say, the opposite is true.

By the end of September we had found placements for 1,482 ex-offenders, 812 of those in employment, 400 in training and the rest in education and community placements. It warms my heart when I work with people like these, and can see the huge change in them as a result of these opportunities. Ex-offenders, as part of our society, are probably one of the most marginalised groups. There are very few voluntary groups that deal specifically with ex-offenders. So it was great to see that those in business would actually give those people a second chance. To me, business is made up of a conglomerate of personal responsibility. We seem to act sometimes as some independent being, separate to humanity and free from control. We tend to forget that most of us who work in business bring our sense of ethics and responsibility to work every day. Why is it acceptable to have a different moral compass at home than at work? I don't believe it is. Surely all of us want to live out our values and concerns wherever possible. I will return to this area later. When deciding what to discuss for this paper, I decided to examine some global trends to discuss the scale of what we are talking about. The one indisputable fact is that globalisation is an inescapable facet of modern life and more than ever before, we are interdependent. I want to consider some figures to illustrate this. World trade has increased fourteen times versus output which has increased six times since 1950. Daily foreign exchange is now at 1.5 trillion dollars. It was 15 billion in 1973. Consider direct foreign investment which affects Ireland greatly and stood at 1.1 trillion dollars in 2000.This exploded from 160 million in 1991. Mergers and acquisitions, right across international borders have increased by 24 per cent in the last decade alone. It is an amazing figure. If we consider multinationals we discover they are responsible for one third of world trade. There are now 60,000 multi-nationals worldwide. There were only 7,000 in 1970 and they are growing in number every day. Each one of those multi-nationals has 600,000 foreign affiliates. Or forget about multi-nationals altogether and just consider large firms. Between 1997 and 2000, the average large firm had 177 alliances with other corporations. Just think of the reach in that. Ireland has its own share of these multi-nationals and large firms. Most are small and medium enterprises, but we are part of a global movement and all our companies are connected in one shape, form or fashion with companies right across the globe. You can see from this the huge reach that business has. What I want to do now is look at the global marketplace, and the global challenges we need to address. Although these figures may be well known to some they are worth repeating for a true understanding of the global scene. 1.2 billion people live on less that a dollar a day. 2.8 billion live on less than two dollars. One billion people are un– or underemployed. By 2025 two thirds of mankind are going to face water shortages. There are an estimated thirty-four million people living with HIV or AIDS but this figure may be much higher. There are 250 million children under the age of fifteen working. So if your home has something other than a dirt floor, you are in the top half of the world's population. If your home has a roof, door, windows, you are in the top 20 per cent. If you have a car, a refrigerator, a VCR, a computer, a microwave, then you are in the top 5 per cent. In Ireland we are golden people on whom the sun shines. Let us look at South Africa today, it has to find ways to give the majority of its citizens a stake in the system by providing housing, education, communications, jobs, and at the same time attract foreign investment. There are many detractors of globalisation and some people even think that globalisation is the problem. I don't agree. Joseph E. Stigletz in his book, *Globalisation and its Discontents*, makes the case that globalisation has been badly managed by the IMF, by the World Bank and by the World Trade Organisations. Western countries like us are hypocritical; we want to compete in all markets, but we don't want others to compete in ours. We ask African countries to live by standards that we ourselves refuse to live by. He makes the point, quite rightly, that Western countries gain disproportionate benefits at the expense of the developing world. Globalisation today is not working for many of the world's poor. It is not working for the environment, for economic stability or to lessen poverty. The actual number of people living in poverty has actually increased by almost 100 million over the last decade of the twentieth century. Let me, after saying all that, make a case for globalisation. Global capitalism has brought huge benefits. Because it has been badly managed doesn't mean we should throw the baby out with the bath water. Mass markets have brought a range of quality goods and services within the reach of a far broader group of ordinary people. Open markets also mean an open forum for ideas. No country has ever had a free market for a long period without being a democracy. And no democracy has ever gone to war with another democracy. Economies of scale have permitted investment of life-saving and life-enhancing technologies and medical breakthrough. Global markets help create better standards of behaviour generally. In addition international companies lift the performance of indigenous business as experienced in Ireland. Technology transfer, through globalization, enhances educational opportunities and creates more efficient work practices as in the area of public administration. Globalisation has reduced the sense of isolation felt in much of the Developing World, and given access to knowledge that a century ago would have been beyond the reach of the wealthiest of nations. Now I want to consider what we can do, as a people, to address some of the issues dealt with above. At its most basic level businesses need to continue to provide employment, because employment alleviates poverty and in most cases it is a pointer towards better prosperity. Companies should also ensure that as well as providing employment, their end products are safe for consumption. I was at a conference recently on Sustainability Ireland, and one speaker, Michael Birmbaum, spoke of a toy produced by Mattel in China which is 97 per cent toxic. It is quite extraordinary that we allow such things to happen. Occupation laws need to be embraced and people need to be trained to a high standard, so that if employment is terminated a new position can easily be found. Environmental concerns need to be tackled further. I am not going to go on about this, because everybody knows that it is one of the major concerns for all. Sustainability needs to be the guiding principle on which decisions are taken. Gender balance needs to be a goal. In 1990, as part of my thesis on Women in Management, I discovered that only 5 per cent of those in management were women. This figure has changed little since then. I was appalled. I went around the universities in Dublin and spoke to women, and said I was a feminist and really wanted to see more women taking charge and adopting more significant roles in business. Those women, who were much younger than me, said that feminism was a dead issue. They believed we had moved on greatly since then and now that so many well-educated women were entering the work force, I would see, in a very short space of time, a revolution at management level. IBEC carried out a similar survey last year and discovered we now have 5.5 per cent of women in management positions. No change at all. Yet the number of women in the work force is now 771,000 which represents 42 per cent of the total work force, of 1.836 million. A stunning figure. But the more I talk to people the more difficult it is to understand why this is the case. But as Mike Cooley suggested in his essay in this volume, more senior women appear to be working for socially responsible businesses which create a social product, so maybe there is research to be undertaken in this area.

With a little effort, we could have openness and transparency as a characteristic of business. Businesses should not hide mistakes, which it does at present. Back in 1960 David Packard, of Hewlett Packard said to his staff: 'I want to discuss why a company exists in the first place. In other words, why are we here? I think many people assume wrongly that a company exists simply to make money. While this is an important result of a company's existence, we have to go deeper and find the real reasons for our being. While we investigate this we come to the conclusion that a group of people come together and exist as an institution so that they can accomplish something collectively that they could not accomplish separately. They make a contribution to society.'

This may sound trite, but it is fundamental. So what does our responsible business look like? I am going to give you some examples which are by no means comprehensive. I have divided them simply by related group. For instance, in relation to ecology and environment, the company should be formally committed to sustainable development. There should be a continuous striving for improvement in relation to the efficiency with which the company uses all forms of energy; it should try to reduce water consumption. Look at the other natural resources and emissions and hazardous substances and try to reduce or, better still, eliminate them. There should be explicit programmes within this company for monitoring energy, water and materials used. There should be an environmental management system. There should be a commitment to using products that are recycled and recyclable, increasing the durability of products and minimising packaging. The company, a good company, should try to balance carbon emissions, with equivalent carbon fixing by planting trees, for instance. In relation to health and well being, the company should have policies to ensure the health and safety of all employees. These policies should be made freely available to all workers. There should be commensurate treatment provided for part-time workers regarding pay, promotion and training. In the area of diversity and human rights, companies should have written policies containing measurable objectives to promote diversity and empowerment in the work force. These should be regularly reviewed against performance. The companies should meet or exceed internationally recognised labour standards and conventions, wherever they operate, including meeting those concerns for freedom of association, the right to engage in collective bargaining, discrimination, minimum wage and living wage. We would expect this of the best companies in the world. Finally, the companies should establish formal mechanisms to maximise promotion in the communities in which they operate.

The community should be seen as an important stakeholder. It should be considered in decision making, and kept informed of the company's operations and plans. The company should focus on critical community issues and use its power, financial and political, to create change. There are lots of other indicators. This is just to give you an idea of what we look for. Let us imagine what would happen if people lived these values and concerns. Business could be seen as the solution to the world's problems and not as the cause. Businesses could use their influence, unique capabilities and grassroots presence for widespread good. Scientists and researchers would be asked to produce products which were not just environmentally friendly, but environmentally enriching. Products would be nutrient-based and they would be compostable. Diversity would be embraced and there would be a place in the workforce for everyone. Inequalities would be frowned upon and eliminated. Equal opportunities would exist regardless of gender or physical ability. People would be proud of the work that they did and the company they worked for. Imagine that instead of working to make profits for a health company, you worked to eliminate health problems throughout the world. Imagine a world where businesses freely admitted their mistakes. Imagine a world where the media were interested in the good that businesses do. Imagine a world where businesses acted as NGOs. Imagine, imagine, imagine. I am going to conclude now because I have gone from what I think is possible in the very short term, to what I really would love to see happen in the longer term. And it is going to happen. Businesses are conscious that staff values are important for the business they work in. Money is not an issue. What you do with your life is now the issue. It is not just quality of life – it's value of life – where we are going, what we want to do with our time here that is coming more and more to the fore. So in conclusion, I want to say that the events of the past two years should bring home to all of us that we are interdependent. That globalisation is a fact of life. There is no going back. With interdependence, there comes a need for collective action, for people around the world to work together to solve the problems that we face, whether they be environmental, economic or political. Global companies, therefore, will need global governments, and as we work towards a system where there is national or international agreements, labels and standards, we should remember that corporate responsibility is really only personal responsibility collectivised.

Imagining the Future for our Schools

CATHERINE BYRNE

Introduction

> 'Emotions'
> I am a volcano, ready to erupt,
> I am a three year old child at a Shakespeare play,
> I am a caged bird, kept away from the world,
> I am a squirrel, in a field of nuts,
> I am a child, at his first day at school,
> I am a dog, trying to learn algebra,
> I am all these emotions bundled in one, but most importantly
> I am a person trying to finish this poem
> Before the teacher kills me.
>   Rory Gleeson

Prior to attempting to imagine the school of the future let us take a moment to reflect on the school of the past and the present because failure to do so will result in building the future in sand. In seeking to reform and renew our schools to meet the challenges of change we need to pause and look at where we've come from and also acknowledge the challenges facing schools today.

Economic Competition and political flexibility, technological innovation, and the Knowledge Society, moral uncertainty and a redefinition of national identity are just some of the features of the global 'change' phenomenon that had swept through Irish society in recent times.

The pace of educational change reflects this radical and sudden transformation of Irish society. Almost since the foundation of the state the education system remained static, constant and predictable. Almost since the foundation of the state a curriculum of cultural nationalism dominated our primary schools and to a large extent, our second level schools. Indeed it is joked that we in Ireland make sure that curriculum change coincides with a change of national currency. If we examine that humorous parallel it indicates that within the last eighty years we have only had two major changes in our education system at primary level – the 1971 Curriculum which paralleled decimalisation and the 1999 Curriculum which coincided with the introduction of the euro.

The economic and social challenges of change mean that business leaders are demanding the education system to deliver particular labour force requirements such as linguistically, scientifically or technologically skilled graduates. Hand in hand with these demands come calls for the system to produce flexible, adaptable and creative individuals in terms of outputs, while at the same time there is an increasing trend by the state towards regulation and standardisation of educational structures.

There is a growing education battleground developing globally in which increasingly, demand for education reform is driven by what can only be described as the international testing movement. Education systems across the globe are frequently compared and contrasted in terms of inputs and outputs by bodies such as the OECD. Here in Ireland we have the annual media fest that accompanies the publication of the *Education at a Glance* indicators which leads to inevitable comparisons of education systems in terms of spending, literacy and numeracy outcomes. Teachers are placed under pressure and feel obliged to compete with the Koreans in one area and the Finnish in another. Indeed this pressure then transfers to pupils. In face of these international trends there is in some countries a retreat behind the barricades as education systems attempt to define and set curricula and standards that are socially and culturally specific to national needs.

The complexity and uncertainty of teaching in the first decade of the twenty first century has led many teachers to focus on the past when expectations were more certain. As teachers grapple with the latest of a series of education initiatives whether it be curricular, evaluative or organisational change there is the inevitable retrenchment evident in phrases such as 'we haven't even begun to implement one change when the next one is upon us' or 'is there no rest from all this change?'. Indeed a cynical view is developing among teachers that if we stand still change will eventually come around to our position.

The School Report

It is against this background that I will offer some ideas about the school, the teacher and education in the future. 'The School Report', to everyone: student, teacher, parent, past pupil conjures up a particular image. The report card is often dreaded not only by students but also by teachers who have to write and defend them and by parents who have to read them! The following extracts from some school reports reminds us how flawed they can be.

PG Wodehouse's teacher wrote that: 'He has the most distorted ideas about wit and humour'. And Woody Allen's teacher helpfully suggested that: 'He seek counselling for his inability to take life seriously'.

If Woody Allen had come under the care of psychoanalyst Carl Gustav Jung he would have met with, if Jung's teacher is to be believed: 'All glib cleverness and humbug'. These light-hearted examples serve as reminders of the challenge to teachers to recognise and nurture the talents of every individual child. However, each child, although a unique individual, shares this earth with billions of other individuals and their capacity to connect with other human beings will determine to a large extent how successful and satisfying their lives will be.

Connectedness

The central tenet of my address, therefore, is to support the importance of connectedness and human contact. The role of educators in schools is primary in developing conected beings, individuals who are in touch with themselves, with the planet they live on and who respect all other human beings and creatures. Life, whatever ones ideology or religion, whatever ones social or economic status, is about contact – physical contact, social contact, emotional contact and intellectual contact – with other people. The opposite is to be disconnected, alienated, isolated.

We come into this world in our own space, the body, and begin life being intrigued with it. Watch babies interlinking their fingers, sucking their toes trying to explore the texture, the taste. When you pick them up they are fascinated with the shape of your nose, the feel of your hair. We are physical beings and love the physical contact of being touched and held. Within the immediate environment of home we begin to make emotional contact and experience the beginnings of intellectual stimulation. We also establish and build social relations within this private world. And we begin to discover the public world outside of the home, usually negotiated with the help of other family members.

Stepping out

Our first big step into the public world, on our own terms, is when we go to primary school. More recently, for many children, play schools and crêches. We enter as individuals and bring all that we have learned and experienced in our homes into this new and 'strange' place, where our formal education begins. Although much has been learnt at home, in this new place we will begin our understanding of the world in a systematic way, beginning perhaps with the key to the secret code of letters and numbers.

As Seamus Heaney describes it in 'Alphabets':

> There he draws smoke with chalk the whole first week,
> Then draws the forked stick that they call a Y.
> This is writing. A swan's neck and swan's back
> Make the 2 he can see now as well as say.

From that first week on we will spend much of our formative years in the hands of teachers. Their challenge and responsibility is enormous.

The OECD report *Knowledge Management in the Learning Economy* puts the challenge bluntly when it states, 'We are moving into a "learning economy" where the success of individuals, firms, regions and countries will reflect, more than anything else, their ability to learn.' The OECD points out that these trends raise 'profound questions for the kinds of knowledge pupils are being equipped with and ought to be equipped with by schools.'

Different countries are responding in different ways to these challenges. The response of Singapore, a small country with a population of just over two million is interesting. The Singapore government takes the view that its future prosperity will depend on developing its people's capacity for learning and dealing with change so they can respond quickly and flexibly, adapting and retraining as future economic opportunities or recessions arise. Singapore's educational vision is of *Thinking Schools in a Learning Nation*. The national curriculum is being cut back, flexibility and creativity are being encouraged, and a number of schools are being established and architecturally refitted as learning organisations.

The Canadian political scientist, Thomas Homer-Dixon says that today's schools and school systems are a tragic example of what he calls an 'ingenuity gap' in society. He talks about the information glut or data smog becoming part of the problem 'as it assails us in ever greater quantities with increasing rapidity'. He claims that in organisations critical to society's economic well-being, key workers may be smarter and able to work faster, but are less wise and less capable of drawing on experience and institutional memory to influence their judgement.

Homer-Dixon argues convincingly that what society needs is lots of ingenuity, which he defines as 'ideas that can be applied to solve practical, technical and social problems, such as the problems that arise from water pollution and cropland erosion. Ingenuity includes not only truly new ideas – often called "innovation" – but also ideas that though not fundamentally novel are nevertheless useful.'

The English futurist, Charles Leadbetter says that the point of education should not be to inculcate the body of knowledge, but to develop capabilities and that the most important capability '...is the ability and yearning to carry on learning.'

In the knowledge society, schools should be the key knowledge organisations, centres of excellence for learning where curiosity, creativity, innovation, risk-taking and lifelong learning are nurtured and encouraged. This should be our aim, not primarily because our economy needs it in order to compete effectively, but because children and adults need it to fulfil their potential, to live meaningful lives and to participate fully in the social, economic and cultural life of their community and society.

The Teacher and the Student
In imagining the school of the future, since they are so inextricably linked in this adventure, students and teachers

must be discussed in tandem. It is important to recognise the needs of both children and teachers. Bryan MacMahon, a schoolmaster from North Kerry, writes:

> ...a good teacher leaves the print of his teeth on a parish for three generations. I realised that each child had a gift, and that the 'leading out' of that gift was the proper goal of teaching. To me a great teacher was simply a great person teaching... If I could only plant a seed in the imagination of each one that would fructify later in each unique individual; if only I could find the gift that I sensed was latent in each one of them: perhaps then I would have fulfilled the purpose of my being a teacher... It became an obsession with me, this sense of deducing from small signals where each one's aptitude lay, even the most seemingly deprived among them.

All good teachers will recognise that moment that MacMahon describes: 'Secretly I often shouted, "Eureka! I have him!" as the tumblers of the boy's mind fell into place'.

If Peter Ustinov had been taught by Bryan MacMahon his school report would not have read: 'He shows originality, which must be curbed at all costs.'

What are the issues for the school of the future?

We need to put more time and money into curriculum design and development. The accelerating rate of social, economic and cultural change demands that the curriculum be reviewed at shorter intervals than heretofore. Curriculum development needs a bottom-up approach from the classroom and the local community with the teacher and the needs of the child at the heart of the process, rather than a top-down approach from the DES.

Teacher Training

A radical new approach to teacher education is long overdue. Paulo Freire reminds us that: 'Those who are called to teach must first learn how to continue learning when they begin to teach.' We need to attract people suited to the job to ensure that we have a motivated and professional teaching force. Careful consideration needs to be given to how best to support teachers in a career in teaching that will embrace high quality initial preparation, induction into teaching and opportunities for lifelong learning at regular intervals throughout their teaching careers.

Students and teachers need a well-resourced environment. This might sound like a basic and unnecessary demand in 2004 in a world class high performing economy, but I'm afraid for many schools, modern school buildings with well-heated, well decorated classrooms, sports, computer and library facilities are far from the reality and very much the dream school of the future.

The school of the future will continue the current trend of transforming schools from a collection of individual classrooms with individual teachers into a community of learners with teams of teachers who are interdependent and equal contributors to the life of the school and the progress of their pupils.

On a national level, we need to transform our education system, which has developed as three separate independent units: primary, secondary and third level, into a far more cohesive and inter-dependent unit and to develop a universal early childhood education and care sector for our very young children. The structure of current state investment in education will have to be reversed so that all our children are cherished equally, beginning with the youngest child. This is a difficult challenge to all the partners in education. While it is possible to identify many 'green shoots' of progress, it is also evident that there are many institutional and systematic barriers to progress which have the potential not alone to stunt growth but prevent it altogether.

I imagine the school of the future will have a holistic approach to the student, recognising the child as an individual with a multiplicity of needs – physical, emotional, intellectual, spiritual, social. A place that helps our young people understand these needs, explore the tensions within – the need to be alone, for example, with the need to have social engagement. Human beings are complex and in the past we have perhaps failed to fully appreciate this in educational terms. We have perhaps concentrated on knowledge and a narrow understanding of intelligence. In this fast moving world our young people must emerge from their years in the classroom as well-rounded, confident members of society not just accomplished products with economic value for the employment market. Freire warns us to guard against the school becoming a 'knowledge market'; the teacher a 'specialist' who sells and distributes 'packaged knowledge'; the learner, a client, who purchases and 'consumes' this knowledge.

Do we want school to be an experience that only teaches techniques and skills for the job market? Job security is no longer about settling into one place for life. It needs constant adjustment to fast changes. To cope with this we need people who can think latterly and who have not forgotten how to be creative. We need to nurture the passion for learning which is innate in human beings. If it weren't for the expression of the innate creativity in human beings we would still be in caves. What kind of person first ate an oyster? A curious one, a risk taker. I fear we may go down the road of quashing curiosity and risk-taking in favour of conformity and unhealthy safeness. Feeling safe is healthy if it gives you the base and confidence to discover yourself, others and this world. Safe is not healthy if it is a cover for fear.

I would argue that at the heart of this model of education is the 'Ever Learning' teacher. Hargreaves identifies many of the challenges faced by the teacher in the modern classroom as:

- expansion and rapid change in the substance of what teachers are expected to teach, making it harder for teachers to keep up with developments;
- expansion of knowledge and understanding about teaching styles and methods leading to a much wider range of strategies from which teachers must select to meet the needs of particular and unique groups of students;
- the need for teachers to work with other professionals in addressing the needs of students;
- integration of special education students into ordinary classes presenting a wider range of abilities and behaviours;
- growing multicultural diversity and increasing recognition of the rights of minorities;
- the problems of physical dropout or psychological disengagement from school;
- changing structures and procedures of school management and leadership, with more emphasis on teamwork and collaborative decision-making.

The advancement of technology

In the midst of change and challenges the teacher must not lose sight of the inherent value of simply being human and being a good teacher. We must learn to experience life to the full with due respect and consideration for other beings and an appreciation for the richness we all bring to each other. No robot or computer will ever provide the rounded richness that a good teacher can bring to a student. If our ideas of education are allowed to narrow and education becomes equated only with the points system, we risk a future where our children stay at home and log on to school via the internet and acquire all the knowledge necessary to pass exams but lose the sense of community and connection and contact that schooling can provide. Learning about human contact is an essential part of education, an essential role for the teacher.

The teacher is the conductor, the lightning rod that takes the wonderful energy and talent of each child and helps her develop according to her own innate blueprint. Children must not be expected merely to conform with our idea of what they should be. By this I mean that we must not project our idea of perfection based on our own experience of learning and success onto our students and our children. As teachers we must learn to teach in ways we have not been taught. Our images of teaching need to be reworked. If our children do not meet our expectations, too often they are made feel 'less than'. 'Making mistakes' is an essential part of learning. Yet we allow little room and show little tolerance for perceived mistakes in our education system. In fact if we were to take the whole spectrum of a life, there is no such thing as a mistake. Perhaps one would have done something differently or made a different decision but one way or another it's all part of life's rich tapestry and one's own individual story. The school of the future in my imagination is a place free of fear, a place where mistakes are not only allowed but their value acknowledged.

The Céifin report on well being and stress in the workplace by Dr Moore found that fear of making mistakes is a great source of stress for employees.

We should talk more to our children about life as it is and the inherent value in every experience. Bryan MacMahon advises that we show our children how 'to say "Yes" to life, to the dark as well as to the bright of it, to its beauty and glory, to its lapses from grace into degradation and its eventual restoration to serenity.' Imagine an educational system in the future whose only agenda was, in reality as opposed to in theory, the full harmonious development of the child.

I want the school of the future to be about passion, real passion, about putting the magic back into learning? Schools should be places that encourage free-thinking and creativity? Shouldn't it be fun? Isn't it a great opportunity to teach people how to carry great ideas lightly, to learn how to enjoy life, how to deal with what is rather than what might be, how to be grateful for what we have instead of coveting what we don't have and believing that happiness is an elusive commodity just around the corner or on the next shelf.

With advancing technology sometimes replacing real contact with nature with a virtual experience, I want the school of the future to encourage children to connect with their landscape, the sea, the flowers, the birds. New technology can enhance those connections. A love of nature nurtured is a lifelong resource. To notice, as Seamus Heaney did in 'The Schoolbag':

> 'And in the middle of the road to school,
> Ox-eye daisies and wild dandelions.'

And of course, the future school will encourage sport and music as an essential part of the curriculum – not as extra curricular activity. And how about ethics, philosophy, human rights? Should we allow more thinking time or reflection time?

Schools do not operate in a vacuum. They are a part of the larger social order. We need to ask questions such as what are society's needs? Does it need conforming individuals for cohesion? Is there a tension? How can we serve the needs of society without trampling on the needs of the individual? The school and the teacher are key elements in education but this is perhaps the first generation that has such strong alternative influences operating outside of the classroom. Many influences are positive; The University of the Library, the University of Travel and the University of the Common Man where each may 'graduate at his or her own pace and to their own satisfaction'.

However, we cannot be passive about the manipulation of young people by commercial interests and expect the teacher to somehow counter these very seductive messages. As a society we need to look at and critique what values we want to live by and look at what supports those values and what undermines them.

Are we becoming a society of consumers and are our values becoming more and more market place values, values of utility and profit? As Freire has observed: 'We do not need advertising to convince us to buy beans or rice, but we do need advertising to purchase this or that brand of perfume and even to buy this or that kind of rice – even if the difference is only in the packaging'.

Are we becoming a society based on fear? Fear is lucrative. It creates demand. It doesn't support a value of just enough. If you don't use x commodity you won't be beautiful with a subtext you won't be loved and will be lonely. If you don't buy y you will not be deemed successful – subtext, society will not allow you in. If you don't buy z you won't be safe – subtext, your physical presence on this earth is under threat. The educator A.S. Neill who established the controversial school Summerhill which allowed children enormous freedom – they could decide whether to attend class or not – said that the school strove to see that 'children are free internally, free from fear, free from hypocrisy, from hate, from intolerance'. Asked why they did not use IQ tests in Summerhill Neill replied: 'They cannot test imagination, humour, creativeness'.

In this materialistic age we risk valuing the excitement of 'things' rather than the happiness of connecting with people. Behind the god of things is emptiness.

What would support the future I imagine?

Because I believe in the pivotal role of the teacher in education in the future it follows that we need good teachers. We need smaller groups of students so that teaching isn't a lecture from the top of the room and other values become lost. We need parental involvement and support in dealing with the outside influences that I have talked about. We need, as teachers, parents, members of society, to realise that children have important things to say and to listen to them.

The school of the future needs to recognise and appreciate that there are multiple intelligences. The most important thing we can give a young person is the confidence to be themselves. If they are secure and feel valued for who they are they will emerge as people connected with themselves and will not need targets for their own lack of self-worth, anger and fear. Not being connected means being alienated.

Racism and intolerance are learnt behaviours. I want the school of the future to be tolerant and inclusive. Inclusion means that the school of the future has no room for bullying or racism. It is a place that respects equality and diversity – the diversity of religion, sexual orientation, disability or different social background. If we believe that society is mirrored in our young people then society must be based on respect – whether it is from different countries, diverse cultural backgrounds or those with disability.

I want schools of the future to be capable of delivering a modern, progressive agenda of equality and inclusion. Teachers cannot do this alone. Tackling exclusion and making inclusion happen takes time, support and considerable expertise on the part of the teacher. Delivery is rooted in reality, not theory. Smaller classes with qualified classroom support will assist inclusion.

In many ways there is less contact between schools and the community now than in the past. Is there a way, for example, of incorporating older members of the community into the school? What could it teach young people? If connection is made with the local community then it is easier to educate about the wider world community, the global village. In these days of globalisation it is important that our young people make this connection. In the past our identity was local, especially in the days before television. While the limits of locality had its drawbacks with the pressure to conform often nipping creativity in the bud, we have to ask, 'In this new global world what is our identity?' With the exposure to a larger world we must develop the confidence to be ourselves and follow our own rich traditions, not to unquestioningly ape more dominant cultures. One of the greatest gifts we can give our young people is the ability to question. In the world of politics and media we must give them the skills to constantly critique the 'story', the consensus behind the story and to ask why.

This relationship between a school and its community, like the relationship between education and society is dynamic and interactive. The school not only reflects its community but is a powerful influence in shaping its development. While our schools reflect a distinctly Irish cultural, social, economic, political and religious past they also take cognisance of the changing nature of society.

In lots of ways our schools are inclusive. In every town and village throughout Ireland children of different social class, different races, varying abilities and backgrounds and beliefs attend school together. But when we scratch the surface we see that while real progress has been made in many areas much more remains to be done. Traveller children have a presence in primary schools but few progress to second level education. International children bring an enriching diversity of language, culture and religious beliefs to schools but because of inadequate resourcing many schools can't meet their needs and teachers are often stretched to breaking point. Children with special needs should also have access to proper educational diagnosis combined with appropriate teaching support and backup.

Inclusivity is more than a tolerance for difference and more than creating a classroom space for difference and having mere presence in school. We must encourage a real and living interaction where children of different cultures, faiths, ethnicities, languages and beliefs are respected and included, not simply preserved and separated. This will not come cheap; it will cost smaller classes, better training for teachers, school support, classroom materials and resources.

The school of the future will also support social inclusion and deal with disadvantage. Inequality in education is at the heart of our failure as a society to break the inter-generational cycle of poverty. Instead of being part of the solution, the education system as currently structured and resourced may be part of the problem. We need action and resources from government to tackle disadvantage. The greatest resource in a school is a qualified, dedicated teaching staff working with smaller groups of children. The link between smaller classes and improved pupil achievement is proven. The American Educational Research Association has shown that smaller classes allow more individual attention and produce lasting measurable gains. No classroom should have more than twenty pupils. For primary school children from disadvantaged backgrounds, smaller classes reduce the achievement gap, lead to higher retention rates, fewer disciplinary problems and more pupils moving on to complete secondary school.

Conclusion

In summing up, let me fall back on an old fashioned teaching technique and aid to memory, the mnemonic. The school of the future can be summarised for me as:

S: Secure, Safe and Stimulating: secure environment for exploring and taking risks; safe physically and emotionally, without fear of bullying or discrimination; stimulating, energising mind and body.

C: Connected, Caring and Creating: connected with people, nature and technology in all their awesome complexities and simple pleasures; caring about themselves and others in a school community that cares about them and their concerns; creativity encouraged and nurtured in its many forms and manifestations.

H: Holistic: responding to the individual's physical, emotional, intellectual, spiritual and social needs; recognising the need for their own space as well as their need for social engagement; responding to and encouraging different types of intelligence.

O: Oasis for Learning: providing a calming environment and friendly facilities for children and adults to step off the fast moving escalator of modern life and reflect on who they are, where they are going and why.

O: Open to Change: providing a proactive rather than reactive response to a rapidly changing world. Leading models of innovation within the learning community and society in partnership with parents, pupils and state institutions. Open to new approaches to teaching and learning.

L: Learning for Life: Embracing the knowledge society as an opportunity for schools and teachers to make a real difference to the quality of people's lives. Not be content with providing antidotes to the crude excesses of consumerist individualism, but welcome the move from brawn to brain as an opportunity to provide for the needs of individuals and society in a way which balances the needs of both.

The school around the corner will never be the same again. And that's no bad thing... for pupils, for teachers, for parents, for society. In the transition from the old bog road to the information highway our schools have played their part, but the best has yet to come.

As I started out with the school report I will end with an overall report on our education system. It has performed well in the past and has the ability to do much better in the future. In shaping that future we should remember Bryan MacMahon's exhortation that 'a school is nothing if it is not a place of laughter and song'.

Imagining the Future for Organised Religion

Archbishop Diarmuid Martin

A few weeks ago I called a meeting at which the majority of priests who work in the Archdiocese of Dublin were to attend. It was an important meeting for a new Archbishop to dialogue about the future. At one stage I wrote in my talk that: 'I have no idea what the structure and distribution of priests will look like in Dublin in ten years time. Parishes will not be as they are today. I have no idea as to what position I will be appointing priests in ten years time. I do not know what new collaborative mission between clergy and laity will eventually look like'.

I asked one of my colleagues to have a look at my text. He came back very happy with what I had written, except with the phrase I have just quoted. He said: 'the priests are coming to the meeting to know what your plan is for the future of the diocese, to hear what is new, and you are telling them you have no idea where we are going! That's not leadership!'

I had thought that the quotation contained something significantly new. I have a feeling that some of my predecessors thought that they knew only too well what the Church would and should look like today and tomorrow and for a long time to come. Expressing uncertainty, I thought, was not only an honest and true reaction, but perhaps also somewhat new.

Organised religion has changed very much already in my life time and it is going to change very much in the years to come. I entered the seminary in Dublin in 1962 and left it after seven years – seven years during which the Vatican Council took place – back into a different Ireland and into a different Church. I left Dublin over thirty years ago and once again came back to a very different Ireland and a very different Church. In the world in which we now live it is essential for individuals, businesses, organisations and churches to recognise change and to act accordingly.

Organised religion will change for good or ill. One thing that is not going to happen is that it will go away. Organised religion is going to be part and parcel of society in one way or another for some time to come. Who would have thought that organised religion would have been such a significant factor in the United States presidential election and in US politics in general at the beginning of the twenty-first century? But even here it is a different kind of organised religion than would have been examined by the electoral pundits of the past; it was not the traditional Catholic or Jewish vote, but something 'neo', something new.

The term organised religion is an interesting one. I have a feeling that in the title that I have been given for my paper, there is a sort of assumption that whereas an 'authentic' personal religion is very important to people, when people begin to organise religion and put up rules, then the whole thing irks a little. For many, organised religion as opposed to a spirituality of personal experience, is somehow less popular, less authentic perhaps – even a distortion of what religion is all about. There is no way, people will say, in which we can put a narrow institutional framework on what are our deepest personal values, on our sense of spontaneous goodness. These cannot be organised, these cannot be commanded; they must be spontaneous if they are to be authentic.

There is no doubt that some kind of private, personal religious sense or sentiment, a sort of spiritual framework within which we can consider our world and draw inspiration, is very appealing to a generation where there is a broad rejection of institution, and is more in favour of expressions of spirituality which are considered authentic and personally satisfying. And there is no doubt that such spirituality would hardly need any organisation at all.

For many, organised religion has been substituted by a secular spirituality of life: a spirituality that is mine personally, one constructed and adapted by me as I move forward in my choices and experiences. Such a spirituality contains nothing of 'the given' and 'the absolute' which is typical of organised religion. Such a secular spirituality may indeed have dimensions of the otherworldly, of transcendent values. It can be nurtured by maxims from the historical religions, but alongside those of contemporary spiritual leaders and contemporary literature it may also draw inspiration from men and women of our time who epitomise in their lives honesty and integrity, courage and zeal for justice.

Secular spirituality can be very attractive. For many it is the only inspiration for a life of rectitude and decency. Secular spirituality can have its litany of its own saints, its own secular icons, its liturgies and celebrations, its music and even its own mortal sins.

It is not surprising then that for many people in Western Europe today organised religion will seem to be not just dull, but too secure, unadventurous, unable to change, with a built-in tendency to defend and perpetuate the institution as institution. Western Europeans are thus surprised and perhaps frightened when they see the joy and vitality of the faith of young Islamic believers.

I will limit myself today principally to reflection on the Christian faith, and especially of the Roman Catholic Church. Jesus himself would be a little surprised to be told that he had founded an 'organisation'. He founded a Church, a Church with sacraments and ministries, a Church which has over the centuries developed organisational structures, just as even the most charismatic movements have. But what Jesus left behind was a communion, a communion of communities which meet together to deepen their understanding of the word of God, to celebrate Eucharist and to support those in need. 'These remained faithful to the teaching of the apostles, to the brotherhood, to the breaking of bread and to the prayers.' (Acts 2:42)

A communion of communities will certainly have organisational dimensions, but it will have to be defined primarily by its purpose rather than by its sociological framework. It is Eucharist, 'that which [we] have received from the Lord' (1 Cor 11:23), which gives structure to the Church. Church is not defined by us, but received from the Lord.

It would be foolish, however, to think that a communion of communities, even with only the minimal structure, will not inevitably be tempted to take on organisational structures very like those which are common in the society of the time in which it finds itself. Organisations inevitably develop a desire to have power or to be close to power. The relationship between organised religion – Christian, Jewish or Muslim – and power is complex and paradoxical. Organised religion tends to drift towards power, it tries to influence power; political power tends to court religion to its side (both President Bush and Senator Kerry were very regular and public Church-goers over the weeks leading up to the recent US presidential election). Yet political power is anxious to prevent organised religion drifting too far towards autonomy, because there is also within organised religion a strong, almost crusading capacity which once released cannot be controlled. Organised religion can be among the most potent factors in fostering either conformity or transformation.

Contemporary Western societies today have an ambivalent relationship with organised religion. On the one hand, there is a rejection of anything which might look like special treatment for the Church which, it is said, should be looked on like any other non-governmental or private body. And yet there is criticism of organised religion if it fails to take up positions – with a prophetic action expected to push the law to its limits – when questions of justice and social concern are involved. Modern secular thought paradoxically asks two questions contemporaneously: on the one hand, 'What is the Church doing here at all?' and on the other, 'What is the Church doing about injustice?'. You cannot have it both ways, however.

Just as historically Church structures have been influenced by organisational models of different periods, office in the Church has sadly often modelled itself too closely on the authority structures of the contemporary secular world, while Jesus himself said quite the opposite: 'among pagans it is the kings who lord it over them and those who have authority over them are given the title benefactor: no, the greatest among you must appear as if he were the youngest, the leader as if he were the one who serves.' (Lk 22:25-26)

People expect different things from the Church in society. Leaders want to use religion. The president of the World Bank said to me: 'The World Bank is the premier wholesaler of ideas on development today, and boy if we could use your retail outlets around the developing world, we could do a lot of good!' Lady Thatcher insisted the Churches should tell people to work harder. After 9/11 in the United States, society turned to organised religion, but there was a sense in which it was to solemnly sing 'God bless America', rather than 'Holy God, We Praise Your Name', to worship God even in times of distress.

When I imagine organised religion in the future, I imagine it then more distant from the structures of power, and thus all the more free to influence power. Looking particularly at the Roman Catholic Church, I see that it must become a Church such that those who look at it, even from the outside, will see not a cold institution, but a community of faith, which is transparent in its beliefs and practices, a community which worships God, but also a community which witnesses to what God is, namely gratuitous love and a caring and forgiving God.

A community which reflects gratuitous love will be an important antidote to a society in which everything is measurable and marketable. It will give witness to the fact that God's love is so great that the believer must respond with a love which goes beyond worldly logic, which goes beyond even enlightened self-interest.

Let me say that that is what Church is today in the lives of many. That is what most people, even those who feel that they will perhaps never again return to be an active part of that community, feel that the Church should be. I spend my time visiting communities around the diocese of Dublin and I encounter a lot of hurt, but I also encounter a great deal of affection and recognition for what has been done and what is being done by Church communities, by individual priests, nuns and lay persons. I encounter parish communities, perhaps with smaller Mass attendance, but which are more vibrant today than at any other time in their history. There is a great buzz around parish life today.

In the current discussions on child sexual abuse by clergy, I feel very strongly that the full extent and nature of such abuse should come to light and that there is no way in which healing can be achieved until that happens. That does not mean that the Church should be blocked from its normal activity of evangelisation and the construction of a more just and compassionate society. Yes, as a Church we have made mistakes. But what we do is much more, much larger than our mistakes and we have every reason to be proud of that 'much more' and we will continue on that path.

However, it would be foolish to think that the Church in Ireland has not lost credibility through the recent scandals. Many have been hurt traumatically. There have been many who have felt their trust betrayed. Trust and credibility cannot be bought or commanded. They have to be earned, and when lost they must be earned again right from scratch.

The first dimension of that earning will be through a renewed witness of integrity, integrity with respect to the real foundations of what the Church stands for, integrity in the lifestyle of individuals and institution. Part of that integrity must be keeping promises of reform made; part of it must be in working towards healing and making people whole. A religion in which God assumed human nature, which teaches that human beings are created in the image of God, must be one which is marked by its ability to enhance people, to give them confidence and self esteem. In the past the Church has stressed conformity, which has the opposite effect, except for some like me whose self-esteem is enhanced by battling with the conformists, or better still, battling with the tendency towards conformity which I find in myself.

The credibility of the Church of the future will come from the credibility of witness. Transparency will be achieved not just through organisational measures of accountability but above all when the love of Christ transpires as the true hallmark of every institution and organisation which bears the name Church.

I would not be honest if I did not say that we have a long way to go. But that also says something about what Church is. Church is a path of conversion. It is the place where one recognises one's sinfulness, but also where one hears a call to conversion, not cheap conversion, but a real change of life, a real desire to follow the good. The Church is an *Ecclesia semper reformanda*: a Church always in need of reform, a community where every member must be ready for conversion.

The future of religious faith must be a faith in the transcendent God, a God who cares and loves and communicates that caring and love in the works of his creation, in the genius of humanity, in the unity of human family and in the integrity of all of creation. Faith in a transcendent God, however, is a faith which, though not insensitive to the realities of the world, is not determined by them. It is interesting that it is very often the less organised religious structures which are the most fundamentalist. Because they lack an integrated doctrine, political expediency rather than the integrity of God's design tends to set standards.

Church will of course remain institution. It will have an organised face. But it will be a very different one from today. I can imagine a future in which the Church is not there in competition with or in a role of substitution for the state in a whole range of services in society. But that does not mean that Church will be absent from society, much less disinterested. Just as in the past, religious congregations emerged to respond to the unmet needs of the marginalised, I can imagine tomorrow a Church which is much more humble, but also much more agile in responding quickly to the community needs which are not met by anyone, and much more sensitive to identifying new social needs in advance.

I might draw attention to two such issues. Firstly, I see a real challenge for all of us in ensuring that, in an ageing population, all will be able to realise their human potential as fully as possible, for as long as possible and in the most dignified way possible. Secondly, we have to address more directly the issue of violence in our society. I am appalled by the number of stabbings which took place in the Dublin diocese over the Halloween weekend. Why do so many young people carry knives? Why is the culture of drinking still so dominant for many young people? Things are not likely to change if we still have areas in the suburbs of Dublin where, as one priests recently told me, there are already three pubs, three betting shops, but no doctor and no pharmacy!

It is very interesting to read of the Church renewal in Ireland in the mid-nineteenth century, after emancipation and quite extraordinarily during the famine. There was a remarkable upsurge of congregations of religious women, which were initially spontaneous groups of women who gathered around charismatic figures who got things done in the face of the poverty of the time.

When we look closer at figures such as Catherine Macaulay or Mary Aikenhead we see that the sensitivity of their response was linked in a special way to a religious sensitivity, even a mysticism which drove them on in the face of difficulties, even difficulties with Bishops. I must say, however, that history proves that the Archbishop of Dublin of the time, Daniel Murray, was a much more outstanding figure than he is often remembered as, especially as at times he took positions quite different from the standard wisdom and different from the standard positions of his colleagues. I hope that my brother bishops will not take this as a declaration of war.

The strength of the Church of the future will depend on how much those who actively adhere as Church members enter into the mystery of what Church is. Where people are not initiated into the mystery of the Church they will always look at the Church only in its sociological structures. On the other hand, if the structures do not witness to the interior mystery, then those structures are the wrong ones and not those which Jesus wished for the communion of communities which he instituted.

To the outsider religion will appear as an organisation. To the initiated it will appear as part of the mystery. Organised religion of the future must be one that is able to engage people of all ages, but especially young people, in dialogue about faith, about belief. It must be one which engages people in their specific questioning about the meaning of their lives and the motives of their hopes. It will be a religion which listens and journeys with people, beginning where they are. It will be less a religion of frenetic doing, than one of leading people to ask the deeper questions.

Faith in today's secularised world will always need community to sustain it. Community will not just be one uniform institution, but a communion of communities, with each community experiencing and sharing its particular path towards God. Christian communities of faith will be places where the mystery of God's love will be celebrated, as revealed in the person of Jesus Christ, who gave himself up that we could be free, that we could be the persons God created us to be, freed from the bonds of egoism and enabled to mirror God's love in our relations with others.

The organisational structure of such faith communities will be different to what we know in Ireland today. But I am sure that they will be strong communities, even though they will be formed by and led by weak human beings. It is the gratuitous love of God which changes us and charges us for mission, not ourselves, not the institution. When we realise that then we can rise above our own limited personal spirituality, rise above the conformity of institution, then we can be fully free to take the leap of faith, to risk our lives knowing that God's love will sustain us.

Imagining the Future – An Irish Perspective

Emily O'Reilly

When I began to put my thoughts together on the topic, 'Imagining the Future – An Irish Perspective' I imagined myself not in the future, but rather in the past, let's say twenty years ago, the year 1984, when although many of us were then into our adult lives was a time very different from today.

So imagine if I or someone like me had been asked to consider what this country might dream of being like in the year 2004. I think I might have said something along the following lines.

Imagine an Ireland where few, if any, of its young people felt forced to emigrate. Imagine an Ireland where immigrants instead came to our shores, seeking our permission to live here, to work and to raise their families. Imagine an Ireland of almost full employment with mainly poorer foreign workers doing the harder, messier, lower paid work, the sort of work *we* used to do in Britain and America. Imagine an Ireland where the majority owned a TV set, and a stereo system, and a fridge, and a microwave and a car and central heating and double-glazed windows and a mobile phone and enough money for a family holiday *and* a spring break.

Imagine an Ireland where an unhappy couple or one unhappy part of a couple was allowed a dignified exit from that marriage through no-fault divorce. Imagine an Ireland where contraception was freely available to everyone; no questions asked. Imagine an Ireland where the stigma of single parenthood had largely disappeared. Imagine an Ireland with a woman President, or better still, two women Presidents. Imagine a powerful, female, Tanaiste. Imagine a brace of female Supreme Court judges, imagine a female Minister for Agriculture, a female Ombudsman, a female Secretary General of a Government Department, a female Assistant Commissioner of the Garda Síochána, a female editor of the *Irish Times*. Imagine an Ireland where the all-pervasive power and might of the Roman Catholic Church had withered. Imagine schools and hospitals run almost exclusively by lay people, imagine the transformation of once great convents and seminaries and mother and baby homes and industrial schools into apartment complexes and car parks and stray bits of motorway development. Imagine Martin McGuinness as Minister of Education for Northern Ireland. Imagine a clutch of Sinn Féin TDs in Leinster House. Imagine Ian Paisley in Dublin for talks with an Irish Taoiseach. Imagine the choice of coffee. Imagine tall skinny lattes, and short robust espressos, and cocoa dusted cappuccinos and americanos with shots, all made by trained baristas and served in great polystyrene cups with special lids and pouring spouts. Imagine Top Shop and Marks & Spencers and Zara and Dorothy Perkins and Miss Selfridge and Next and Tesco and Sunday shopping and twenty-four hour shopping seven days a week. Imagine waiting lists for Hermes bags and eye creams. Imagine a second fashion floor in Brown Thomas. Imagine the Kildare bypass, and the Drogheda bypass, and the Athlone bypass and the restoration of tram lines in Dublin, and bus lanes and dirt cheap air travel and great big cars with DVDs on the ceiling and windows that go up and down when you tell them to. Imagine the ending of the plastic bag epidemic. Imagine smoke free airports and bus terminals and shops and offices. Imagine smoke free pubs. In Ireland.

Imagine all of that and imagine what you might have said in response. You would have said, 'Emily, that would be paradise.' So, ladies and gentlemen, welcome to paradise.

Here we are, twenty years later, in the paradise we might have imagined some twenty years ago and I ask myself; why are we still whinging? Why after that gargantuan transformation of public and private life in a direction that many of the country's most thoughtful and concerned citizens wished for, is there still an enormous disquiet about the nature of our Irish society and the sort of people we have become?

Let us assume that it was God we had entreated for all those things. How would God react now, in the face of that huge, Santa sack of gifts to us, to the fact that we're still not happy? We all know the old Chinese proverb about being careful what you wish for and the poison that can seep through answered prayers. That is part of the reason. It is also bound up with the fundamental law of physics that to every action there is an equal and opposite reaction or, perhaps more appropriately, unexpected reaction. Another reason is that perhaps the tyranny of poverty and oppression, albeit relative in Ireland's case, has been supplanted by the modern, cutting-edge tyranny of wealth and freedom. A fourth reason has to do with our still faulty understanding of human nature.

Many of us, if we have any developed sensibility, recoil at the vulgar fest that is much of modern Ireland: the rampant, unrestrained drunkenness, the brutal, random violence that infects the smallest of our townlands and villages, the incontinent use of foul language with no thought to place or company, the obscene parading of obscene wealth, the debasement of our civic life, the growing disdain of the wealthy towards the poor, the fracturing of our community life, the God-like status given to celebrities all too often replaced somewhere down the line with a venomous desire to attack and destroy those who were on pedestals the week before, the creation of 'reality' TV, more destructive in its cynical filleting of the worth and wonder of the human soul than anything George Orwell could have imagined.

'But it wasn't meant to be like this,' we will protest. Divorce was meant to be for the deeply unhappy, not the mildly bored; drunkenness was supposed to be practised by the down and out and the marginalised, not the boys and girls with cars and careers and more prospects than their granny could shake a stick at.

More cars were supposed to help people get around, not force them to sit in line through the full two hours of a drive time programme at motorway exits, motorways which, incidentally were *also* supposed to help people get around. Bypasses were supposed to relieve bottle necks not shuffle them forward to the next 'unbypassed' town. Portlaoise was never meant to be a West Dublin suburb.

Sunday shopping was supposed to be a convenience for the harassed worker, not a new religion. We still haven't worked out exactly what we thought 24-hour shopping was supposed to do, but still can't get over that vaguely depressing feeling we experience whenever we think of shops with lights on at 3am and, more importantly, of the people who have to work there.

And yes, I suppose we did seek to curb the power of the Church, but that didn't mean we wanted to empty the churches themselves, or reduce seminaries and convents to advertising fodder for the property sections. And while the nuns had their problems, it would be nice if the odd one were still around to lecture our daughters about the evils of the micro-mini and the bared and pierced midriff, or to knock the odd hospital consultant into shape with the menacing flutter of a wimple. And while we greatly welcome the challenge of choosing from a choice of 179 assorted types of coffee in the morning, we didn't mean for Bewleys to go.

But let me make something clear at this point. This is not a middle-aged lament for the good old days. Or perhaps I should say it's not *just* a middle-aged lament for the good old days. I may well think that Dublin's Financial Services Centre is over endowed on the tall skinny latte front, but it is still a hell of an improvement on what was there before, the poverty laced slums that were the Sheriff Street tenement buildings.

Irish women's lives have also been transformed immeasurably over the last twenty years; our children have opportunities unimaginable two decades ago; luxuries denied to all but the wealthy are now available to the masses; good political choices have been made that have broken the poverty cycles of many, many families; the stultifying cosh of the Catholic Church has been removed and we at least can see ourselves in our new spiritual nakedness and use occasions such as this to ponder what we have become and what we want to become.

And what we have become, it seems to me, are participants at what we would have called in my teenage years, a free house, but this time on a massive scale. Released from the handcuffs of mass religious obedience, we are Dionysian in our revelry, in our testing of what we call freedom. Hence the staggering drink consumption, the child-like showing off of helicopters and four-wheel drives and private cinemas, the fetishising of handbags and high heels, the inability of some to contribute to charity without a photographer on hand to record it, the supplanting of bog-standard childhood ailments like measles and whooping cough with fat induced obesity and diabetes.

I ask the question; 'Who or what is the real us?' Were we real when we were modest in our habits, and daily communicants, and mass mass attendees, and self-effacing contributors to charity, and energetic participants in voluntary work or are we real now as we either indulge in, or look enviously upon, the phenomena I have just described?

Is not the speed at which we have jettisoned so much of our religious practice in particular suggestive of a society that was not so much spiritual as spineless, cowed by the power of the Church, observing what we observed out of fear rather than faith? The challenge in the short-to medium-term, I would humbly suggest, is how to take and accept this newly secular society and inject it with a value system that takes from the best of that which we have jettisoned and discards the worst. We must grub down in the national drain and retrieve the baby from the bath water. It is a challenge equal to that posed by a puzzled head scratching uber-liberal commentator some years ago when he observed that he and many like him had spent years attempting to get rid of the hard rocks of fundamental Catholicism from the field that was Ireland. That, he noted, had now been done, yet all that was left was an empty, sterile, barren patch of land. What, he wondered, do we do with it now?

So let's re-imagine Ireland. Let's take it as read that our economy is going to chug along reasonably well for at least the next few years. Let's take it that we have enough retail outlets and baristas and mobile phone ring tones and botox providers. Let's examine instead what makes us truly human, what makes us 'happy', what the pursuit of the latter should entail. Let's fundamentally imagine all of ourselves on our deathbeds, forced as we would be at no other time, to examine our souls and the lives we have lead. A friend of mine likes to say that in order to lead a good life we should also imagine what we would like to have said about us at our funeral. He has a check-list. That check list includes, that we were good to our families, that we subsumed some personal ambition to the needs of those around us, that we contributed at work if we worked outside the home, that we contributed to the community and that we left some child at least better off for having known us.

Most of you here will subscribe to that, but are they necessarily the values that our children are imbibing from the social, educational, cultural and political ether that they are exposed to. The wealthier we become, the more the air is sucked from our collective spirit. Let us examine what lies behind the pursuit of happiness. Those of us who grew up in the sixties and seventies and who were educated in Catholic schools, will have been reared with the notion that happiness is not something to be attained in this life. With the passing of that era, and the coincidental massive increase in personal wealth, we are now awash in the notion that not alone can happiness be attained this side of paradise, but that the more money you have, the more of the happiness stuff you can buy. Hence the big cars, the private jets, the Manola Blahniks, the cosmetic surgery, the botox and so on. What we appear collectively to have failed to grasp is that happiness is as serendipitous as lady luck, as ephemeral as star dust, as likely to be granted to a child perched on a gutter in Calcutta as a Hollywood star arrayed on a red carpet on Oscar night.

Money can't buy you happiness, but if it is so patently true why does this modern Irish society stubbornly refuse to accept that truth. Those of you who read a recent *Sunday Times* article (31/10/04) would have got a flavour of this phenomenon of excess in a front page report in which a Dublin retailer was exulting in the fact that her outlet was now coping with a waiting list of five hundred women in pursuit of a hand bag that retails at €5,000 plus. 'It's great,' opined the retailer, 'for the country.' Imagine that on your obituary, 'Here lies Mrs X, fifth in line for a Birkin bag, and raging she wasn't first.'

Let me read to you the observations of one marvellous man, a man, who in his winter years really is contemplating his life and what it has taught him and what he wants to pass on to those who will listen. The man is John Mortimer, the creator of Rumpole and the following appears in his new book, *Where There's a Will*:

> I'm writing this at a good time of the year. The beech trees are covered with fresh, green leaves; we are going to have a birthday lunch in the garden. My grandchildren will play in

birthday lunch in the garden. My grandchildren will play in the mysterious sunken copses, disused flint pits now filled with tall and ancient trees, where I also played as a child. The daffodils will be in flower and the dogs will be jumping over them. There is every possible reason for happiness; but it's also a moment of sadness too. How many more such birthdays will there be? It's sad my mother never saw Rosie and Emily, my daughters, grow up. Although (the poet) Shelley was right about our sincerest laughter being fraught with sadness, it's the sadness, in a way, which makes happiness complete.

There is a story about a devoted fisherman, in love with the sport, who went to sleep and found himself, on a perfect day, fishing in a clear stream. Every time he cast he hooked a fine salmon. After this had happened a dozen times in succession he asked the gillie where he was. Was it, perhaps, heaven? No, he was told, it's hell. Happiness too often or too regularly repeated becomes misery. And here perhaps we're getting near to what happiness is for me. Happiness is a by-product. If it's sought for deliberately, desperately it's elusive and often deceptive, like the distant sight of an oasis.

So what, towards the end of his life are Mortimer's values? Despite his fame, despite the memories of his stellar career as barrister and author, despite his wealth, despite all those material things, it is the simple joy of his garden, of his children and of his grandchildren, of ritual, that resonates in the final chapters of his book and of his life. In his book, Mortimer also takes us through many of his own epiphanies, life-lessons that guided him through to the melancholic, but ultimately fulfilled state in which he now exists.

All of us have those epiphanies; the trick is to recognise and to use them. The national trick is to pray for a national epiphany that will kick start us into a view of life and how it should be lived in a way that doesn't start in the car park of Liffey Valley and end in the inner mall of Blanchardstown.

I have had a number of those epiphanies, not all of which I have acted on but some of which I would like to share. I had an epiphany when I caught myself and two of my daughters kneeling in front of a two metre long shelf of facial cleansers in the new monster Tesco in North Dublin, paralysed by the great God of market choice.

I had an epiphany when, in the busyness of my work life last month, I failed to notice a little piece of paper in the window of my littler daughter's classroom announcing the Junior Infants Halloween hat competition thus ensuring that Ella went to school on the appointed day with a hastily wrapped piece of newspaper around her head while the children of the more engaged mothers outdid Philip Treacy with their millinery.

My daughter, God bless her, didn't even notice, and she walked around on the hat parade like the late Queen Mother at Ascot. I never would have risen to the three foot tall Cat in the Hat structure one mother produced, but I had still missed out on the pleasure that will never be repeated of getting down on the floor with my Junior Infant child and imagining and attempting to make a wonderful hat. My loss. Lesson learnt.

But those are personal stories. What are the epiphanies we should imagine here today for this country, and how do we do it this side of our dotage, before hanging, so to speak, concentrates our minds?

It would be good if we recognised the new religions of sex and drink and shopping for what they are and tiptoed back to the churches. It may not even be necessary to believe, it may be sufficient just to remind ourselves of some of the universal truths about charity and decency and how to live a good life, all of which are contained in the teachings of the major religions. It would be good to regain our sense of the magic of ritual, of the year marked by rites and rituals, not the seamless, joyless blending of undifferentiated weekdays. It would be nice to get the summer over before the Christmas displays begin.

It would be good to insert ourselves into the lives of our community, reawaken our sense of what we can contribute, but also what we can receive, the preciousness of belonging, of being caught up in something stronger than your own individual self.

It would be good to discipline our children by disciplining ourselves, to realise the risks of jaded appetites, of needs too quickly and too elaborately met, of lives made too cynical, too aware through the imposition of distorted adult views of what constitutes happiness, to realise also that the new impoverished are not those without the DVDs and the latest Playstations and mobiles and private cinemas and the cut down Fendi bags but those perhaps, who have them and who got them without the slightest personal effort, every wish and expectation delivered upon without striving, without time to dream, without that peculiar joy known as delayed gratification.

What we also need to do as a country rapt in love as we are with market forces and consumer products is to begin again to speak the word that increasingly dare not speak its name in this thrusting, strutting, alpha male society – poverty. It still exists, in the literal sense, in the sense of individuals and families existing on bread and chips, strung out on stress and worry, their feelings of isolation and inadequacy made all the worse by the apparently effortless garnering of wealth and decent lifestyle by those around them. Twenty years ago, poverty was just as nasty, but made more bearable perhaps by a cultural acceptance that it was part of what we were. Now the term 'loser' commonly used, piles psychic pain onto the literal pain of being poor.

It also exists in the spiritual sense as I have outlined. It exists in our failure to date to imagine a wealthy country that strives for more than the satisfaction of needs we never knew we had until the multinationals created demand. Political debate too often is about personalities, cultural debate currently revolves around the physical siting of a theatre rather than the role of theatre and music and poetry in breaking down the poverty of spirit I have spoken of. Piping Mozart into the sound systems of our junior schools, teaching marginalised adolescents how to play a musical instrument, seeing art as central to our lives and our spirit rather than a luxury extra accessed by the few would do much to improve our civic life. Let's debate that and worry not about the Abbey.

There is moral poverty; the staggeringly swift creation of a society in which we are increasingly neutral in our judgements of all sorts of objectively bad behaviour, be it infidelity, the abandonment of families, loutish behaviour on the sports field, underage sexual behaviour. Those who indulge are, bizarrely, more likely to be feted than condemned. Punch someone's lights out, wreck your head with Class A drugs, and you're more likely to appear on a chat show than a court bench.

A young female pop star comes to Dublin and puts on a sexually explicit show in front of a theatre packed with sub-teens, brought along, incredibly, by their mothers and fathers. One commentator described such displays as the mainstreaming of the pornographic imagination; what was previously top shelf is now at gymslip level.

I am conscious as I read this that little if any of what I am saying is new. The wealthy are frequently vulgar and prone to showcasing that which they have accumulated. That was as true centuries ago as it is today. Tolerance levels for all kinds of behaviour wax and wane depending on societal norms, the role of the Churches, the historical context, and a myriad other factors. The poor will always be with us, and human greed will triumph, like a dodgy stock option, when the higher virtues are suffering a bit of a slump.

So why do we even bother discussing it? Why not sit back and wait for tides to turn, stop banging our heads against the brick walls of smugness, complacency and massive self-satisfaction that are all around us? The answer lies in what I have struggled to explore in this paper – our humanity, the belief that sometimes people want to do better, be better, and think of people other than themselves. The deeply heartfelt hope that our children will have better lives, and in the context of this shiny new wealthy Ireland, that that better life has to do not with the accumulation of stuff, but with an awareness of the true meaning of a rich life, of a life where the pleasures of love, of companionship, of reading, of art, of sharing one's gifts, of seeking to attain ever higher understanding of the mysteries, beauties and even ugliness that surround us, are really all that matter.

Many of these problems of our age may seem like so much trivia, the aesthetically unpleasant downside of a vulgar, decadent Western lifestyle, the pious handwringing of those who also benefit from that decadence. But how we are as a people, how we treat each other, and particularly how we treat our most vulnerable, informs our relationships with other cultures, other countries. It can inform issues of foreign policy, of international aid, and every area where we interact particularly with countries that cry out for our help.

Self-absorption, the relentless pursuit of the material hardens our hearts, closes us off to those who need to share our gifts. It can happen on a personal level, it can happen on a national scale. Equally though those small personal epiphanies can also begin to impact nationally, and we should be as conscious of the trickle up effect as the trickle down, of the impact of mass individual actions, mass individual decisions to re-engage, to rediscover the spiritual, rediscover each other and examine and take on board the truth of what makes us fully human.

Last night, my hat-wearing Junior Infant daughter was chanting the chorus of a little song that may sound mawkish in this grown up adult setting but has a resonance nonetheless. She sang, 'And in this world of darkness, we all can shine a light, you in your small corner and I in mine'.

I am loath to imagine concrete things for the next twenty years. The supermarkets are already full to bursting. Let me imagine instead the creation of a new discourse, where a safe place is created to talk again about values, about the spiritual, where the political class summons the courage to shift its focus even slightly away from the purely economic and focuses instead on what else really matters, what the people they serve need for a full and generous minded life quite apart from tax breaks, toll roads, and airline terminals. Let us imagine the spirit of Céifin as the dominant one, let us imagine nothing less than the decentralisation of the national soul from Dublin to Ennis.

Imagining the Future – A Global Perspective

Michael D. Higgins

May I begin by saying that many people today experience a great longing for authenticity. They sense that at a personal, community and global level they have experienced a frustration at best, perhaps even a violence that condemns them and others to a life far short of their capacities at an ethical or creative level. Such a very strong statement is one that is very particular to this present age but it is one that has engaged scholarship at different periods in different centuries in a very powerful way. For example, there is a particular moment when the spiritual gives way to the rational and the Enlightenment arrives. There is a particular moment when modernism arrives, but what one can detect in the present period is a deep search for authenticity and a sense of frustration that it is not being realised.

One of the distinguishing characteristics of the present time is that there is a greater intolerance to the discussion of such a contradiction and such a problem than at any time since I started as a student or as a university teacher. It is a time of narrowness. It is a time of extreme intolerance and it is a time of a very, to my mind, reduced scholarship. I list, therefore, a set of issues I propose to deal with that I have been thinking about since I was contacted to give this paper. I will give a summary of what I am suggesting and then return in more detail to some of them.

I am suggesting that we cannot live fully conscious lives unless we question the inevitabilities that are suggested to us. This involves developing both the personal and social consciousness necessary to create a critical capacity so that we might truly experience freedom and choice and moral responsibility for the consequences of our actions. Second, I suggest that in dealing with that kind of challenge, we will find no automatic solution in retreating to old certainties. This does not mean that the certainties have been discarded. I am simply suggesting, philosophically, that they are insufficient. For example, I spent time as a young student in the 60s and 70s in the United States, Britain and Ireland, when we were told that the Western world was an advanced world and it was only a matter of time before the rest of the planet lost its backwardness and could become modern and developed just like us. The fact was of course that this set of assumptions constituted a model that was ethnocentric. As a model it was culturally insufficient and in sociological terms as a theory of change unacceptable in its assumptions, its methodology, and above all in its conclusions. Historically, it also lacked credibility, a fact that didn't seem to bother many people. It spawned a host of works, and a kind of scholarship that was unilinear, evolutionist, and accepting of political and economic structures that were in political, economic and cultural terms dominating, exploitive and manipulative.

It is very interesting the way waves of intellectual ideas return. I recently met a person I knew in the 60s and 70s while studying in the United States. I met him on a plane and he was heading to what was the Soviet Union after 1989. As he put it, he never thought those old files would be useful again. He had dug them all out and here he was peddling the modernisation model all over again. The basic ideas, which had been provided in a series of studies known as the Princeton Studies between 1958 and 1963, were being recycled uncritically. That is what I mean when I say that some contemporary scholarship is shabby.

I turn now to the need for questioning inevitabilities and the certainties, that are not necessarily sufficient to deal with this angst of our times. I think the way people handle the problem is very interesting, but escapist. I say so with great respect. People change beliefs and have done so in the history of ideas, through the constructions of myths. The nature of a myth is such that you suggest something is so obvious that it is natural for it to be taken for granted, rather like modernisation, as I had described it from the Princeton Studies; this was a powerful myth. There was no person who studied at post-graduate level in the United States in that period from the end of the 1960s to the end of the 1980s who wasn't reared within this myth. Globalisation is a contemporary related myth. When you look at the assumptions of globalisation that you have a single model of the economy to be prosecuted in a linear way, market-led and so forth, private rather than public driven with no notion of involvement of the state and unmitigated by social protection, one can see that globalisation too is a myth. The difference between it and the modernisation myth is that it is being implemented through institutions which were not originally set up for such a purpose, such as the IMF, (and although there is a crucial difference between them) and the World Bank. Joseph Stiglitz has critiqued that difference between the IMF and the World Bank, but it is a myth. The difference between such a myth and others is that it is a dangerous myth. Where it is most dangerous is that it dulls critical capacity.

What does one do when invited within twenty-four hours to deliver a paper? Certain books will select themselves. I found myself reaching for Carl Jung's book, *Modern Man in Search of a Soul*. When I reflected on the Jungean thesis in this work it suggested to me something that is also in my poems by the way, the notion of exile. The past from which we have come is embedded in us – in our psyche, in a way from which we cannot totally distance ourselves. We also look to the future, as to how we might see it as promise or hope. But how do we handle the present then as we take ourselves from the past and face the future? In the discussion where Jung makes his critique of Freud and Adler, he suggests a crucial difference between them. Freud approaches this problem almost as if our condition was pathological. In the case of Jung he leaves the possibilities of consciousness there for our realisation. The concept of consciousness is incredibly important, I suggest.

In relation to my opening statement, that we experience a longing for authenticity, consciousness tells us that it doesn't matter enormously where it is institutionally located, simply that spirit cries out for a version of the self and of the world, and for the capacity for creation that is not being met by our present circumstances. We have to answer that problem through an integrated scholarship that is not easily available to us anymore. It is as if we try to see these problems through a broken glass, through pieces and shards of experience. Thinking it through raises a question about the role of culture – culture which is at once inherited and being recreated, but also fundamentally charged, never static. Creativity is not something that is located randomly and vicariously in individual people, like those phrases 'she had it in her', or 'the piano will stand to her,' suggest. The alternative view is that we are all potentially creative, if allowed to develop. Genius may be more randomly and vicariously distributed.

Accepting the necessity and power of creativity has implications for our discourse on the economy. I have been at many conferences on the knowledge economy and I repeat something that I have taken to repeating in the hope that it would lodge somewhere, and it is that the creative society makes possible myriad forms of the knowledge economy but if you change the society to one form of the knowledge economy in a short period of time, you not only damage your capacity economically, but you dislocate the creative society and you diminish the capacity for a vibrant citizenship. This is something that has to be taken seriously because it has wider implications such as the relationship of education to the economy at every level through the economy. If today you state that, you are as an academic, in favour of reflective scholarship, this somehow or another is to confess a disability in the current times in relation to funding. I was an academic for most of my life. I have taught in the university system in America, in Britain and here. I am distressed at what I see is as this lack of confidence in the possibility of hope at an intellectual level.

In previous decades scholars seemed so much more morally engaged. If I were to go back to Jung's work in 1933, before World War II, scholars were trying to envisage a time where we would never have war again. Then through the sixties and seventies, an immense debate arose about what you might call the enframing of technology and science. There was a debate about the bomb. There was a debate about the use of physicists in creating instruments of war, about whether or not science was neutral and all of its relation to technology.

The story, of course, is not a black one entirely. One of the greatest developments through the last twenty-five years has been an increasing interest in ecological responsibility. Even at the UN Conference in Rio, you had the Business Council for Sustainable Development deciding sustainable development was an unavoidable concept.

Looking back at the origins of a dangerous hubris, the high point of an uncaring science was perhaps when Francis Bacon said: 'I leave to you Nature and all her children in bondage for your use', and again of nature, 'We must gouge out her secrets'. Francis Bacon, at the beginning of a period of empire and colonisation was supplying a rationalisation for these forces and a relationship to the environment which would be tragic in its consequences. It was a frame of mind, a paradigm, a governing myth. So we are searching, therefore, for a new paradigm in which we might enframe science and technology, and at the same time discover or rediscover, points of continuity from the past and be able to face the future without fear.

The problem is one of having an instinct for what ought to be, what might be, and finding it contradicted. In this regard I suggest it is worthwhile considering the concept of prophecy. In one of the poems in my new collection, I deal with this concept of exile. We are in exile, I suggest, from the different and perhaps better versions of ourselves. It is rather like the situation in the Psalm, when a person cries out to God and asks: 'Why do you not answer?' It is that we have in ourselves, a hunger for a better version of ourselves and to have that better version of ourselves made available. Our cry is perceptible but we wait for the answer. Whether you call this in a political sense a longing for Utopia, a better place, or strictly speaking, a different place, or whether you call it, in a theological sense, prophecy, it is a cry out of exile for a possibility that has not been rejected, even if it appears unattainable, in present circumstances.

It is interesting that Martin Luther King, who was not to see the full realisation of his dream in the United States, described his vision spatially, 'I have been to the top of the mountain', and then he described it prophetically: 'I have seen the promised land'. My poem concluded that the resolution of our problems has to be achieved by ourselves.

One of the most important aspects of change in our contemporary lives has been the change in the relationship between economy and society. Our attitude to work and leisure has been crucially changed. A new discourse has been invented to justify our subservience to the economy. Issues of personal and social development have given way to ones of utility. We rarely hear such questions as, 'What would you really like to do with your life? Where do you think your interests really lie?' On the other hand we are instructed on a daily basis as to what we must do with out lives and our children's lives to sustain 'the needs of the economy'.

Our society is under pressure for time. Voluntarism is declining. There is little time for community. Time previously spent with neighbours is spent in traffic jams. We earn more, but everything costs even more. The relationship between the generations is fundamentally changed with care of the elderly, for example, now being discussed almost entirely in terms of institutional provision. We now have 65.1 per cent of women and 1.5 per cent of people above the age of sixty-five in the workforce. There is hardly anybody else to be sent into the economy.

If you contrast the present discourse to that which prevailed when I was appointed first in 1969 in UCG, as it then was, NUIG as it is now, we were being endlessly invited to attend seminars about the leisure society, what were we all going to do when there was so much free time – take on hobbies, learn languages, travel? People were to prepare themselves for retirement. I remember quoting Oscar Wilde's phrase 'work is for horses'. The working life was to be shorter. The working year was to be shorter. The working day was to be shorter. Then suddenly there was no free time. Now it is a disloyal and near traitorous act not to work endlessly. You are letting the economy down if you retire at seventy. When you now consider the time spent either at or travelling to work there is very little free time left.

A solution to our form of economy has to be structured across the spectrum of space and time. It has to take into account the issues of income but also issues of quality of life. The challenge is to sustain the economic version you desire at the same time finding a way to realise our ethically unrealised selves.

We began most of our lives when the concept of citizenship was being widely debated. With citizenship came notions of universal rights. Surely people should be entitled to clean water... Surely people should be entitled to education.. Surely people should be entitled to good housing... Surely people should be free from insecurity in illness or in old age... But now we listen to lectures about how we should purchase our own security in every one of these areas. We are becoming consumers of services that will more and more be provided to us by the market rather than as rights we are entitled to under a concept of citizenship. The same French company that provides water to those of the black community in California is providing it in South Africa. In fairness to the South African government they are trying to get them out and get back to some concept of provision.

Such a world as I have described has been accepted as our inevitable world. This world sustained by the myth of globalisation is a world about which we have to ask ourselves a fundamental question, Do we have the critical capacity to subject it to critique? We have in our consciousness actually shifted to being consumers rather than citizens. This is accompanied by the commodification of more and more aspects of life and it has created an alienation that has masked itself as a sole desirable lifestyle – a lifestyle that invites us, I suggest, towards a life of being consumed in one's consumption. The interdependency which was at the basis of citizenship is recognised but it is devalued by an aggressive and indeed, I suggest at times, vicious individualism. Indeed I notice our language itself has changed. People rarely speak about 'the personal' anymore, but speak instead of 'the individual'.

Market fundamentalism, I have suggested, is accepted as the single paradigm of economic development and its imposition as the sole strategy for development and poverty alleviation. This I suggest is disastrous and not only in the poorest countries or transition economies, but also in the so-called developed world.

We have as consumers experienced such a dulling of our consciousness as blocks our capacity to critically engage with our world. If we take the media as an example, we are affected by fragmentation of audiences, concentration of ownership, and a drive towards cultural homogeneity. We should be honest and accept that the concentration of ownership in the media internationally, with its stress on commoditised entertainment on television in particular, plays a crucial role in this limitation, even destruction, of our life world.

Our scholarship has become apologetic and accommodating rather than critical. We are, as Charles Taylor, the Canadian philosopher puts it: 'acquiescing in our own unfreedom'. We are 'drifting', as he puts its, to our 'unfreedom'.

This broken world appears to us in shadows through the shards of experience and some of the most insightful and ethical responses that do engage with this condition, do so on a single issue basis. I found, for example, and this is even more controversial, that some of my friends, who became communitarians in the eighties in California, did not want a strong role for the State, the bureaucracy. Let's all do it, make the changes, from the bottom up. Ronald Reagan as Governor, clasped his hands and said thank you for helping me. He closed the parks. Nettles grew where flowers grew before. Some well meaning reformers had assisted the agenda of the right without thinking about it.

Again, one of the fastest areas for growth in bookshops, not only here but all over Europe, and particularly in North America are self-healing books, which raises the question : Can you heal yourself? The answer in such writing, is of course that, you must heal yourself first and then you deal with the wider world. I suggest that much of this is a very insufficient response to the kind of problems which I have been describing. Of course, it is important to recognise the significance of personal integration so as to survive in a broken world, but we need to attend to the urgency of an integrated approach to our shared interdependent planetary existence. We have, to invert a Raymond Williams phrase become the targets of consumption rather than the arrows of a deeper more extensive and humane communication. We have the technological capacity to widen and deepen our communication and engage with all of the issues of the world and with other people from different cultures. Instead of such a project taking place the technology has been turned against us. Even in the production values of television programmes context is eliminated and a distrust of narrative is obvious. There is a distrust of the possibility of democratic extension. The world, in the new value system, is one whose complexity is amenable solely to expertise. The view it sustains is that such an expertise is separate from ordinary democratic discourse. Ordinary people, it is suggested don't understand. From this assumption it is a short distance to the dangerous views of Leo Strauss with his notion that the public may have to be deceived and the concept of the 'noble lie' as adopted by the Neo-Conservatives in the recent history of the United States.

I remember writing a poem once which reflected on authoritarianism in the church in rural Ireland in the 1950s, when people accepted that priests had often to read books for the benefit of the general public who were unable to understand. It was for the good of your soul. Many people objected to that of course. Nobody, however, objected in the eighties and nineties to people asserting that economists have to tell you what the state of the economy is, for your sake, because you don't understand it. The structure of a television programme on the economy in that period was to interview members of the public who could be assumed to give a simplistic version of a problem. Then, when they were finished, the three or four eminent people who understood the economy were wheeled out. They summarised it for you and told you how it really was. The Church in Ireland in my lifetime was never as unaccountable as the spokespersons for an unacceptable and morally disinterested economics such as was emerging then, and would come to prevail, almost exclusively, at the present time.

It is appropriate therefore, to ask the question as to what kind of world we inhabit. Why do we accept it? What are the consequences of appearing to recognise an interdependency that we are forced to contradict? As we discard ethics for a narrow marketed fundamentalism can social cohesion survive in such an atmosphere of exclusion and market fundamentalism? In Mrs Thatcher's Britain, one of the fastest growth areas was in private security firms. You had very wealthy homes in gated communities which they felt needed protection because of their perception that the underclass were coming up the road and, as the new rich from Mrs Thatcher's speculative economy put it, 'they want what we have and we are protecting ourselves against them, because we know what they want and they are not getting it'.

The acceptance of a world so divided, a planet that is not sufficiently respected for its diversity, places much at risk. It has a numbing effect. People regularly say to me that they are not happy about this or that and they want to do something about it, but they lack the moral resources and the courage to actually debate it. All I want at the present time is to simply raise some questions that I feel to be important, but that are neglected. Going back to Jung's work, he spoke about the unconscious and then about the practical consciousness that enabled one to do tasks, but more importantly, of a discursive consciousness, which was one where you allowed yourself to ask the questions: Why am I doing this? What are the reasons behind this?

In Jung's example, Westerners thought it absurd and unnatural that tribes people in parts of Africa believed that if you shot an animal, a dying person in a neighbouring village may be robbed of his or her soul. Yet how much more ridiculous and unnatural was it for visitors to be overdressed in the tropical heat and to require their servants to wear white gloves over their black hands?

So there is a problem about what is natural. That phrase: what is natural purports to describe what is inevitable and make the myths by which we live. I have been to many places where there are huge problems with poverty, disease and malnutrition. The question digs itself into you. How often do we have to see this and experience it again and again on television? Doesn't it really contradict any ethical or moral impulse we claim to have within us, when we insist that many things repeat themselves as if they were inevitable.

In 1994 the late and brilliant Erskine Childers, who was an assistant general secretary of the United Nations, wrote in his book, *Renewing the United Nations*, that, '1.4 billion people now live in absolute poverty, 40 per cent more that fifteen years ago, nearly one in every four human being alive today is only existing on the margins of survival, too poor to obtain the food they need to work, or adequate shelter, or minimal health care, let alone education for their children... overall for the poorest among human kind, the thirty years that is between sixty-four and ninety-four have been like trying to go up a down escalator'.

Our structures of Aid Trade and West, our Neo-Liberal market model assures the continuity of these divisions. In 1960 the richest one fifth of the world's population enjoyed thirty times more than the income of the poorest fifth. By 1989, the richest fifth was receiving sixty times the income of the poorest. Aid has been falling every year for the last ten years. In relation to trade, what is being transferred from the South to the North every day remains unfair. I say this in relation to debt. If debt had been cancelled in 1997 for the twenty poorest countries the money released for basic health care could have saved the lives of about 21 million children. By the year 2000, the equivalent of 19,000 children per day.

Take Zambia for instance which in 1989 paid in debt service, a sum that was 13 per cent of its gross domestic product. It was greater than the combined health and education budget. For every 1 per cent you transferred from debt service to the combined health education product, you would have been able to save the lives of children at the level I have mentioned. In that country, life expectancy due to HIV and AIDS has fallen from forty-three years to thirty-three years, with half a million children out of school and the education system in collapse. We created an agenda in September 2000 through the eight Millennium Development goals, about which there should be no backsliding. At the present time one of the eight millennium goals that deals with Africa and HIV and AIDS, is at about 42 per cent of what was hoped for. This is less than half of the money committed in Johannesburg and it is something like forty-two billion short of what is needed to address that problem.

I want to finish by saying this about our unquestioning acceptance of the world in which we live. If we had wanted to live fully conscious critical lives, if we had wanted not to be the target, if we had wanted not to have the arrows directed at us, as consumers, if we had wanted, as Raymond Williams put it, to be the arrow not the target, would we have accepted so much of the monopoly I mentioned earlier in the media?

Between 1987 and 1989 the ubiquitous Rupert Murdoch, through his news corporation earned 2.3 billion dollars. He paid no corporation tax, and in the whole world, for all of his operations, he paid less than 6 per cent tax? Do we regard that as a good thing? Why do people put up with all of this? Well, Tawney the historian speculated once about why tadpoles put up with their miserable existence? 'Maybe it is because they live in expectation that one of their number will sprout a jaw and leap to earth and become a frog.'

There is a suggestion in our society that through some kind of individual miracle we can escape from our condition. What is needed is a return to questioning the inevitabilities by which we live, looking at some of the certainties discarded, not in terms of sufficiency, critiquing the myths by which we live, concentrating on the critical capacity that the scholarship requires and that public debate requires, encouraging consciousness, respecting prophecies.

The capacity to change our world still exists and we can create rather than remain the victims of history. One of the most inspiring phrases in Raymond William's latest book, *Towards 2000*, 'Once the inevitabilities are challenged we have begun to gather our resources for a journey of hope' reminds us that we too can take our first steps towards a new world.

CÉIFIN CONFERENCE 2005

'Filling the Vacuum?'

A panel of local, national
and international speakers will

- Pose questions
- Debate issues
- Explore solutions

AT THE 8TH ANNUAL CÉIFIN CONFERENCE

West County Hotel, Ennis, Co Clare
8th - 9th November 2005

For further information please contact Susan at
The Céifin Centre for Values-Led Change,
Shannon Business Centre, Town Centre, Shannon, Co Clare

Tel: 061 365 912 • Fax: 061 361 954
ceifinconference@eircom.net • www.ceifin.com

Are we forgetting something?

'Romantic Ireland's dead and gone, it's with O'Leary in the grave', was the poet's cry a century ago. On the cusp of the third millennium many people fear the death of the Irish sense of community. The concept of a caring society seems well-buried in the selfishness of consumerism and *mé-féin*-ism encouraged by the phenomenon of the Celtic Tiger.

These were the concerns that inspired Fr Harry Bohan to organise a conference on the theme 'Are We Forgetting Something? Our Society in the New Millennium' in November 1998. Topics addressed ranged from the human search for meaning, to the economic boom in context.

This provocative and incisive volume, ably edited by Harry Bohan and Gerard Kennedy, also includes the views of the three chairpersons of the conference: Marie Martin, John Quinn and Michael Kenny, and is interspersed with well-chosen poetic and spiritual reflections on the topics addressed.

ISBN 1 85390 457 0

€11.45

Are we forgetting something?

Our society in the new millennium

Edited by Harry Bohan & Gerard Kennedy

Working Towards Balance

There is growing consensus that corporate and market values now shape Irish society.

Economic growth is synonymous with progress. But economic activity represents only one facet of human existence. Its values are not the only values that prevail in society. As we begin a new millennium, our society must be challenged to wonder what direction it is taking. There is an obvious need to ensure that the agenda of the corporate world and the welfare of local communities can co-exist in a meaningful relationship.

These are the concerns that were addressed at the *Working Towards Balance* conference in 1999, organised by Rural Resource Development Ltd, (now the Céifin Centre) the papers of which are published in this book.

ISBN 1 85390 474 0

€11.45

Redefining Roles and Relationships?

'These annual conferences in Ennis are establishing themselves as an important date in the calendar and meeting a need for serious discussion about major social and ethical issues of the day.'

Mary Robinson
United Nations High Commissioner for Human Rights

The papers presented at the third Ennis Conference in 2000 are collected in this book. The need to redefine roles and relationships in a rapidly changing society was examined in many areas of modern life.

Papers include: 'Contemplating Alternative Relationships of Power in a Historical Perspective', Gearóid Ó Tuathaigh; 'Rebuilding Social Capital: Restoring an Ethic of Care in Irish Society', Maureen Gaffney; 'Rise of Science, Rise of Atheism: Challenge to Christianity', Bill Collins; 'Social Justice and Equality in Ireland', Kathleen Lynch; 'Putting People at the Centre of things', Robert E. Lane; 'Why Are We Deaf to the Cry of the Earth?', Seán McDonagh; 'It's Just the Media', Colum Kenny

ISBN 1 85390 526 3

€11.45

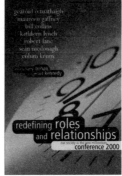

Is The Future My Responsibility?

Have we become helpless in the face of change or can we manage the future? More and more people talk about the emptiness of modern life, they wonder where meaning is coming from and what values are shaping us; they say it is not easy being young today in spite of the choices and the freedom. We cannot assume that if we simply sit back and comment the storm will blow over, or that we will return to the old ways. The fact is we are experiencing a cultural transformation, we are witnessing the passing of a tradition, the end of an era. Every day we hear questions like 'Why aren't they doing something about it?' or 'Who is responsible for this, that or the other?' It is time to ask: 'Have I got any responsibility for the way things are?'

Including contributions from Nobel laureate John Hume and internationally renowned writer and broadcaster Charles Handy, *Is the Future My Responsibility?* is the fourth book of papers from the Céifin conference, held annually in Ennis, County Clare, and published by Veritas.

ISBN 1 85390 605 0
€12.50

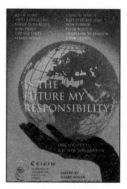

Values and Ethics

can I make a difference?

What are the values that we choose to prioritise and live by? What price are we prepared to pay for ethics? Is it enough to rely on the law as the minimum standard of acceptable behaviour? Ultimately, can one person make a difference?

These and other far-reaching questions are addressed in *Values and Ethics,* the fifth collection of papers from the Céifin conference which is held annually in Ennis, Co. Clare. Contributors include Professor Robert Putnam (author of *Bowling Alone*), sociologist Dr Tony Fahey, Bishop Willie Walsh and Dr Lorna Gold from the University of York.

There is a belief in Ireland that we have not adjusted to our new-found prosperity. In a society that measures almost everything in monetary terms, values and ethics are increasingly sidelined. We now face the challenge of taking our social growth as seriously as we take our economic growth.

This book gives hope that real change can begin with committed individuals who believe passionately that shared values can become a social reality.

ISBN 1 85390 658 1
€13.95

Global Aspirations and the Reality of change

how can we do things differently?

Just imagine experiencing a feast of story ideas, dialogue, music, drama and good conversation...

Just imagine being transported through the revolution that Ireland has experienced in the past decade – the rise and rise in consumption, the acceleration in the pace of work and personal life, the effect of communication replacing transmission, the means overcoming the end ... but despite all that, imagine that change is possible. Imagine a revolution of deceleration...

'Indifference will not be allowed', imagine the challenge of these five words!

Just imagine having a whole morning to reflect on the possibilities of influencing the system of power that keeps us politically docile and economically productive. Imagine the joy of realising that power is present in every moment, in every relationship and there is ultimately no 'small act'...

Just imagine all that and the camaraderie and the energy of spending two days with three hundred people who want to do things differently, who want to effect change. Imagine conversations – at early and late hours – stories, dreams, ideas, debate, energy.

Power within. Céifin 2003. Just imagine!

ISBN 1 85390 000 0
€13.95